Read People Like a Book:

How to Analyze Understand, and Predict People's Emotions, Thoughts, Intentions, and Behaviors

By Patrick King
Social Interaction and Conversation Coach at
www.PatrickKingConsulting.com

Table of Contents

Introduction

Have you ever met someone who seemed to just have a natural gift for *getting* other people? They appear to be blessed with an instinctive understanding of how other people tick and why they behave as they do, to such an extent that they can often predict what they'll say or feel.

These are the people who know how to talk so that others really hear them, or the people who can quickly detect when someone is lying or trying to manipulate them. Sometimes, such a person may perceive someone else's emotions and understand their motivations to a degree that even exceeds that person's insight into themselves.

It can seem like a superpower. How do they do it?

The truth is that this ability is not really anything mystical, but a skill like any other that can actually be learned and mastered. While some might call it emotional intelligence or simple social awareness, others may see it as more akin to what a clinical psychologist or psychiatrist may do when they conduct an intake interview with a new patient. On the other hand, you may see this skill as something that a seasoned FBI agent, private detective, or police officer may develop with experience.

In this book, we're going to be looking closely at all the ways we can develop these skills in ourselves, without needing a psychology degree or any experience as a trained CIA interrogator.

Reading and analyzing people is no doubt a valuable skill to have. We encounter and interact with other people constantly and need to cooperate with them if we hope to have successful, harmonious lives. When we know how to quickly and accurately analyze someone's character, behavior, and unspoken intentions, we can communicate more effectively and, to put it bluntly, get what we want.

We can adjust the way we communicate to make sure we're really reaching our intended audience; we can spot when we are being deceived or influenced. We can also more easily comprehend even those people who are very different from us, and who work from very different values. Whether you're trying to learn a little more about a person you've just met by snooping in their social media history, or interviewing a new employee, or trying to understand whether the mechanic is telling the truth about your car, reading people well is a priceless skill to have.

It's crazy when you really think about it: every person you ever meet is essentially a mystery to you. How can we really know what is going on inside their minds? What they're thinking, feeling, planning? How can we ever really understand what their behavior means, why they are motivated as they are, and even how they see and understand *us*?

Another person's world is like a black box to us. All we have to go on are things *outside* of that black box—the words they say, their facial expressions and body language, their actions, our past history with them, their physical appearance, the tone and quality of their voice, and so on.

Before we go much further in our book, it's worth acknowledging this undeniable fact—human beings are complex, living, changing organisms whose inner experience is essentially closed off inside of them. Though some might make claims otherwise, nobody can really state with any certainty that they know who somebody is completely.

That said, we can certainly become better at reading the observable signs. "Theory of mind" is the term we use to describe the ability to think about other people's cognitive and emotional realities. It's the (perfectly human) desire to make a model about someone else's thoughts, feelings, and actions. And like any model, it's a simplification of the depth and complexity of the real person in front of us. Like any model, it has limitations and doesn't always perfectly explain reality.

Our goal in learning to fine-tune our capacity to analyze people is to make best guesses.

What we learn to do is gather as much high-quality data about a person as we can, and analyze it intelligently. If we can input these small pieces of data into a robust and accurate model of human nature (or more than one model) the output we can obtain is a deeper understanding of the person. In the same way as an engineer can look at a complicated machine and infer its operation and intended function, we can learn to look at living, breathing human beings and analyze them to better understand the what, why, and how of their behavior.

In the chapters that follow, we'll be looking at many different models—these are not competing theories, but rather different ways of looking at a human being. When used all together, we gain a fresh understanding of the people around us.

What we do with this understanding is up to us. We could use it to foster a richer and more compassionate attitude to those we care about. We could take our knowledge and apply it in the workspace or anywhere we need to cooperate and collaborate with a wide variety of different individuals. We can use it to become better parents or better romantic partners. We can use it to improve our small talk, to spot liars or those with an agenda, or to reconcile effectively with people during conflicts.

The moment we encounter someone new for the very first time is the moment we most need to have well-honed powers of perception and analysis. Even the least emotionally and socially intelligent people can learn something about other people if they engage with them long enough. But what we're focused on in this book is primarily those skills that can allow you to gather genuinely useful information about near-strangers, preferably after just a single conversation.

We'll dig a little deeper into mastering the art of a snap decision that is actually accurate, how to make appraisals of people's personalities and values from their speech, their behavior, and even their personal possessions, how to read body language, and even how to detect a lie as it's happening.

Another caveat before we dive in: analyzing and reading people is about much, much more than simply having hunches or knee-jerk emotional reactions about them. Though instinct and gut feeling may play a role, we are focused here on methods and models that have sound theoretical evidence and seek to go beyond simple bias or prejudice. After all, we actually want our analyses to be *accurate* if they're to be any use to us!

When we analyze others, we take a methodical, logical approach.

What are the origins or causes of what we see in front of us, i.e., what is the historical element?

What are the psychological, social, and physiological mechanisms that sustain the behavior you're witnessing?

What is the outcome or effect of this phenomenon in front of you? In other words, how does what you're seeing play out in the rest of the environment?

How is the behavior you're witnessing triggered by particular events, the behavior of others, or even as a response to you yourself?

In the chapters that follow, we'll look at smart ways to structure your rational, data-driven analysis of the complex and fascinating people who cross your path. You may start to appreciate how this kind of analysis is at the root of so many other competencies. For example, knowing how to read people may improve your capacity for compassion, boost your communication skills, improve your negotiation abilities, help you set better boundaries, and the unexpected side effect: help you understand *yourself* better.

Why You're Probably Doing it Wrong

Many people believe they're "good with people."

It's very easy to boldly claim that you understand another person's motivations, without ever really stopping to check if you're correct. Confirmation bias, unfortunately, is a more likely explanation—i.e., you remember all those times your assessments were correct and ignore or downplay the times you clearly got it wrong. That, or you simply never ask if you're right in the first place. How many times have you heard, "I used to think so-and-so was such-and-such kind of person, but once I got to know them, I realized I was completely wrong about them"?

The fact is that people are often far less accurate judges of character than they like to believe. If you are reading this book, chances are you know that there are a few things you could probably learn. It never hurts to start a new endeavor on a blank slate. After all, nothing can get in the way of learning truly effective techniques like the conviction that you know everything already and don't need to learn!

So, with that in mind, what are the obstacles to becoming brilliant at reading people?

Firstly, the biggest thing to remember is the *effect of context*. Maybe you've seen a listicle online to the effect of "5 Telltale Signs Someone is Lying," and went on to see if you could spot any in real life. The trouble with this is obvious: is the person looking up and to the left because they're telling a lie, or has their attention simply been caught by something on the roof?

In the same way, a person making an interesting "Freudian slip" in conversation could be telling you a juicy secret about themselves—or they could simply be sleep deprived and literally just made a mistake. Context matters.

In the same vein, we cannot take a *single* statement, facial expression, behavior, or moment to tell us something definitive about the whole person. Have you not already done something today that, if analyzed alone, would lead to some completely nonsensical conclusions about your character? Analysis can only happen with data—not a single datum—and it can only happen when we are able to see broader trends.

These broader trends also need to be situated in the cultural context that the person you're analyzing comes from. Some signs are universal, whereas others can vary. For example, talking while your hands are in your pockets is looked down upon in most cultures. Eye contact, on the other hand, can be a tricky affair. In America, eye contact is generally encouraged because it is considered a sign of honesty and intelligence. However, in places like Japan, eye contact is discouraged because it's thought to be disrespectful. Similarly, a set of cues may mean one thing in your own culture, and something entirely different in another. It can be slightly difficult to remember these different models of interpretation initially, but as you practice the art, it'll start coming to you naturally.

If a person does the same unusual thing five times in a single short conversation, then that's something to pay attention to. If someone simply claims, "I know that woman. She's an introvert. I saw her reading a book once," you wouldn't exactly call them a master at unraveling the human psyche! So, it's worth remembering another important principle: in our analysis, we *look for patterns*.

Another way that smart people can come to not-so-smart conclusions about others is if they *fail to establish a baseline.* The guy in front of you may be making lots of eye contact, smiling often, complimenting you, nodding, even touching your arm occasionally. You could conclude that this guy must really like you, until you realize that this is how he is with every person he meets. He in fact is showing you no interest above his normal baseline, so all your observations don't quite lead where they ordinarily would.

Finally, there's something to consider when you're studying other human beings, and it's often a real bind spot: yourself. You might decide that someone is trying to deceive you, but completely fail to take into account your own paranoid and cautious nature, and the fact that you were recently lied to and are not quite over it yet.

This final point may ironically be the real key to unlocking other people—making sure we understand ourselves at a bare minimum before we turn our analytical gaze outward. If you're unaware of how you may be projecting your own needs, fears, assumptions, and biases onto others, your observations and conclusions about others will not amount to much. In fact, you may have simply discovered a roundabout way of learning about yourself and the cognitive and emotional baggage *you're* bringing to the table.

Let's see some of these principles in action.

Let's say you're interviewing someone your company intends to hire. You have only a short time to determine whether she'd fit in with the rest of the team. You notice that she's talking quite quickly and occasionally stumbling on her words. She's sitting literally on the edge of her seat, hands clasped tightly together. Could she be a very nervous and insecure person? You suspend judgment, knowing that everyone is nervous in interviews (i.e., you respect context).

You notice the candidate mention more than once about how her previous employer was very demanding with time, whereas she prefers to work independently and manage her time herself. You wonder if this means she's poor at taking direction from management, or if she genuinely is a more independent and proactive type. You have no baseline, so you ask her about her university days and what she studied. She tells you about research projects she conducted independently, and how closely she worked with her old supervisor. This tells you that she *can* work under management . . . if the project is something she cares about.

If you had only focused on her nervousness, you wouldn't have gotten very far. Many recruiters will tell you that speaking ill of a previous employer is hands down a red flag, but in the interview, you look for *patterns*, not single events. You may even consider that she may be acting nervously because *you* are making her nervous. You might know that by being a tall and physically dominating person with a deep voice and a serious expression, what you are witnessing is not the woman herself, but the woman as she appears in your company.

By remembering a few simple principles, we can ensure that our analysis is always contextual, well-considered, and three dimensional. It's about synthesizing the information we have in front of us into a coherent working theory, rather than simply spotting a few stereotypical behaviors and coming to easy conclusions.

The Problem of Objectivity

"Your cousin was really upset when you made that joke about politics last night."

"Upset? No, he wasn't upset; he thought it was funny. I remember!"

"No way! He was frowning. I thought he was totally mad at you . . ."

Have you ever been in a conversation with a group of people, only to later find out that different members of the group had a completely different assessment of what happened? Sometimes, people disagree entirely on whether someone was flirting, whether someone was uncomfortable or offended, whether someone was feeling off or being rude. It can feel like you were living in two separate realities!

Some studies show that only about seven percent of our communication comes from actual spoken word, whereas a whopping fifty-five percent of it stems from body language. This means that what people say is often the worst indicator of what they actually want to convey. Even their tone of voice only tells you about thirty-eight percent of the actual story. One can now see why people often leave group conversations with contrasting opinions on what really took place in that interaction—they're using the wrong factors to arrive at their judgments. To grasp the real, non-verbal conversation or dialogue that someone is engaging in with you, you need to consider both their verbal as well as non-verbal cues.

We've already seen that simply claiming you're a "people person" is not really proof that you are factually any better at reading them. But it turns out there may be a scientific way of actually measuring this quality in people. Simon Baron Cohen (yes, there is a relation to comedian Sascha Baron Cohen—they're cousins) has devised what he calls a social intelligence test. The test is scored out of thirty-six, with results lower than twenty-two observed in those with autism, and the average score being around twenty-six.

The test essentially asks you to infer other people's emotions by *simply looking at their eyes*, i.e., it tests how empathic they are. The person may be smiling, but are they actually feeling really uncomfortable? Knowing how to read other people's emotions has been linked to overall higher social intelligence, which then links to better cooperation on teams, empathic understanding, and better people-reading skills.

If you're curious, you can do this test yourself on a desktop computer by following the following link:

http://socialintelligence.labinthewild.org/.
You'll be asked to look at pictures showing
just people's eyes and to choose from four
emotions to describe what you think the
person is feeling. But be prepared to be
surprised by your results—or the results of
your friends and family.

Of course, this is a test that has flaws and
limitations like any other test of this kind. If
you're a social genius but have poor
vocabulary or are not culturally Western or
an English speaker, for example, your
results should be interpreted with caution.
This test shows you how good you may be
at reading people's emotions from very
little information—i.e., from nothing more
than a single glance at their eyes.

But this is only a small piece of the puzzle.
What this test tells us is that we do not all
possess the same range of social skills, and
perhaps that we may be less adept than we
first thought. This in turn shows us that it's
not always enough to go on hunches or
intuition—you may easily make the wrong
assessments of people.

When dealing with things like the murky, hidden inner depths of other people's hearts and minds, we need to make efforts to remain as objective as possible. We cannot always trust our first impulse. If you did the test above and scored only twenty-six out of thirty-six, then you could reasonably conclude that ten out of every thirty-six encounters would have you incorrectly interpreting someone's facial expression.

If that's the case, what else are you missing?

On the other hand, the look in someone's eyes is just a tiny portion of the information you have to work with in any social situation. You have their posture and body language, what they say (and what they don't say!), their tone of voice, their attitude, the context in which you are both having a conversation . . .

If you didn't score very high on the test, don't worry, it doesn't mean that you're autistic or completely socially unaware. In real life, we encounter much more in a passing moment than just a single frame image of someone's eyes alone. You may actually be better at piecing together this and all the other information at your disposal than you think.

What you might like to try, however, is to deliberately work to improve your people reading skills in the ways discussed in this book, and come back a month or two later to re-take the test. You may discover something fascinating—that our empathic and social skills are not fixed but can be developed and improved upon. Once you've got your baseline for your own people-reading skills, we're ready to move on to the theories and models that will help you refine your skills to Sherlock levels.

Takeaways

- Most of the communication that takes place between people is non-verbal in nature. What people say is often a poor indicator of what they want to convey, which makes people-reading a valuable life skill with almost endless benefits. Although we're all blessed with different aptitudes, it's possible to develop this skill in ourselves, as long as we can be honest about where we're starting from.

- No matter which theory of model we use to help us analyze and interpret our observations, we need to consider context and how it factors in. One sign in isolation rarely leads to accurate judgments; you need to consider them in clusters. The culture people come from is another important factor that helps contextualize your analysis appropriately.

- Behavior is meaningless in a void; we need to establish a baseline so that we know how to interpret what we see. This means that you need to ascertain what someone is normally like to detect deviances from that to draw accurate interpretations of when they're happy, excited, upset, etc.

- Finally, we become great people-readers when we understand ourselves. We need to know what biases, expectations, values, and unconscious drives we bring to the table so we are able to see things as neutrally and objectively as possible. We must refrain from letting pessimism cloud our judgments because its often easier to arrive at the more negative conclusion when an alternate, more positive one is equally likely.

- To gain better insight into the progress you make as you read through this book, you need to know your proficiency at analyzing people as you start out. Simon Baron Cohen has come up with a test available on http://socialintelligence.labinthewild.org/ that'll help you gauge how good you are at reading people's emotions right now. It is also a good way to come to the realization that we are perhaps not as good at reading people as we think we are.

Chapter 1. Motivation as a Behavioral Predictor

Why bother to understand people at all? Why go to the trouble of learning about how people operate and why?

If you think back to any situation in which you were desperately trying to get a read on someone, it might have been because you were very invested in how they would *act*— or else, trying to understand why they had already acted as they did.

To understand why people behave as they do, we need to examine the causes and drivers of that behavior: their motivations. Everyone (including you) is driven to act for some reason or other. You may not always see or understand that reason, but there is one. Only insanity has a person acting for no reason at all! So, to get a grip on any behavior, to understand it, predict it, or even influence it somehow, you need to understand *what is fueling it*, i.e., you need to understand what motivates a person.

Why did you pick up this book? Why did you get up this morning? Why have you done any of the no doubt hundreds of things you've already done today?

You had your reasons, conscious or unconscious, and another person might gain considerable insight into who you are by knowing what those motivations were.

In this chapter, we're going to look at everything that inspires human beings to act: desire, hate, like and dislike, pleasure and pain, fear, obligation, habit, force, and so on. Once you know what motivates someone, you can start to see their behavior as a natural and logical extension of who they are as a person. You can work backward from their actions to their motivations, and finally to *them* and who they are as individuals.

People are motivated by psychological, social, financial, even biological and evolutionary factors, all of which could interact with one another in interesting ways. What do people care about? Asking about interests, values, goals, and fears is more or less asking about motivations. Once you know where a person is coming from in this sense, you can start to understand them and their world *in their own terms*.

In this chapter, we'll explore the many different motivators behind human behavior. Think of these as explanatory models through which you can observe the behavior of others and use to understand what you're seeing, on a deep level. Let's start with the deepest level of all: the unconscious.

Motivation as an Expression of the Shadow

It's an old cliché: a bald and overweight middle-aged man zooms by in an expensive, noisy red sports car, and people on the sidewalk remark, "Gee, I wonder what he's compensating for?" It's just a coarse joke, but it speaks to a common understanding of the fact that sometimes people are driven by unconscious, inner forces that they may not necessarily see themselves.

You may be familiar with Swiss psychologist Carl Jung's concept of the shadow. To put it very simply, the shadow contains all those aspects of our nature that we have disowned, ignored, or turned away from. These are the parts of our being we hide from others—and even from ourselves. Our pettiness, our fear, our rage, our vanity.

The idea is that when we integrate our shadow, we cultivate a deeper feeling of wholeness and can live as authentic, complete human beings. You see, Jung didn't care about "positivity" and self-improvement in the sense that's popular today. He thought that psychological health and wellness came from acknowledging and accepting yourself—*all* of yourself—rather than in pushing the unwanted parts of yourself further and further away.

It can be enormously gratifying to do "shadow work," i.e., to consciously attempt to reclaim those disinherited parts of yourself. But how can we use this concept to help us better understand those around us, who also possess shadows?

The thing about the shadow is that even though it's pressed out of conscious awareness, it still very much exists. In fact, it may make itself known in more subtle ways, manifesting itself in behavior, thoughts, and feelings, or appearing in dreams or unguarded moments. If we can observe and understand these outward signs in others, we can gain a deep insight into their character.

We live in a world of duality—dark exists because of light, we only understand up because of down, and what is high energy must eventually slow and stop. Simply understanding this principle can help us understand people, too. We are all a blend of complementary, connected, and interdependent forces. Like the yin yang, each gives rise to and balances the other.

Imagine someone who was raised in a strict household and pushed to do well academically. No late nights, no drinking, no friends over, only study all day every day. You could look at such a person and notice how profoundly unbalanced or polarized their being is. Their conscious mind is focused on only one aspect of their being. But what happens to their impulse to be free, to rebel, to play, to be a bit wild? Where does it go?

You probably know a few people who lived childhoods exactly like this. And the way the story goes may seem very familiar: in early adulthood, such a person finally succumbs to the long-repressed and hidden needs for freedom, expression, and rebelliousness, and "goes wild," abandoning their studies and living it up almost as though they were making up for lost time.

We can understand this phenomenon by using the principle of the shadow. Even if we encounter a perfectly well-behaved and disciplined student, we know that their shadow contains everything that is unacceptable to them, to others, and to their environment. In the same way that it takes energy to constantly keep a beach ball submerged underwater, it takes energy to deny the shadow. But eventually, the ball pops up.

Living with a shadow that is unknown to us can cause us psychological discomfort. The mind, body, and spirit seeks to be whole, and if this wholeness is only achieved through an explosion of repressed material to the surface of conscious awareness, then so be it. By using Jung's theory of the shadow, you can achieve a few key insights when it comes to understanding people.

First, you can develop a deeper understanding of why they are as they are, and this inevitably leads to heightened feelings of compassion. If you know that the bully at school learned in childhood to suppress out of awareness all his own feelings of inferiority, weakness and fear, you can see his behavior with a measure of understanding. You are able to engage with him beyond a superficial level—you are dealing with all of him and not just the carefully curated conscious self that he is portraying on the surface.

Second, by using the shadow model, you allow yourself to reach out to and communicate with people far more effectively. Although every one of us is a divided being, there is nevertheless an impulse toward wholeness and authenticity. If you can speak directly to those unacknowledged parts of a person's psyche, you are able to communicate more deeply.

For example, an arrogant, narcissistic person may have a shadow filled with self-hate. In that shadow is everything they cannot bear to acknowledge about themselves, so much so that they deny that it's even a part of them. The common reaction to narcissistic people is to want to tear them down, to laugh at them, or to resist their claims of grandiosity. But this only strengthens the feelings of shame that created the split in the first place. If you can see a person's grandiosity as essentially a defense, you can adjust your communication accordingly.

Granted, you cannot get someone else to acknowledge parts of their own shadow simply because you think they should, but it can certainly give you an insight into how to deal with them in the future. A final way of using this theory to understand others is to see how the shadow is projected to the outside world.

The shadow is filled with painful, uncomfortable feelings. We relieve this pain and discomfort by ignoring or denying the feelings, and what better way to disown them than to claim they belong to someone else entirely? Shadow projection is when a person unconsciously attributes his own shadow traits to another person. For example, someone who feels intellectually inferior may find themselves calling everyone and everything "stupid" or haughtily criticizing the efforts of others.

Though on the surface they may have styled themselves an intellectual, you can see what's really going on: the mask of cleverness is there to protect real feelings of inferiority. If you happen to be called stupid by such a person, you know that it has nothing to do with you and everything to do with them.

You could use this understanding to be very persuasive or even manipulative—for example, complimenting the person's intelligence when you want to flatter them.

You could also use your insight to generate deep, compassionate understanding. For example, you could try communicating to this person that there is nothing shameful about being "stupid" and that you accept and love them whether they're intelligent or not. This helps integrate the shadow—if the repressed material is not felt as shameful and uncomfortable, there's no need to push it away anymore. It's like relaxing the pressure on the beach ball and allowing it to float gently to the surface.

None of this is to say that we need to go into intense psychotherapist mode every time we meet someone new. Integrating the shadow is long, difficult work that cannot be done on anyone else's behalf. The best thing we can do for ourselves is work hard on our *own* shadows while we use it to help us acknowledge and understand the workings of other people's shadows.

You might even start to look at your own culture a little differently—groups can have their own collective shadow. What are the things that your family, community, or even nation refuse to acknowledge as a group about themselves? And how does this help you understand their resulting behavior a little more?

In the Jungian spirit, the most helpful and healing attitude to adopt when it comes to the shadow is one of love and acceptance. Be curious but be kind. Your goal in identifying someone's (possible) shadow is not to catch them out, to get a one up on them, or to figure out a button you can push for your own gain.

Instead, it's about *seeing wholes* in a world that is often split, broken, divided, and unconscious. If you can see the shadow in operation in someone else, it's also an invitation to look honestly inside ourselves.

Once we can look at another person's shame, fear, doubt, and rage with acceptance and understanding, we can do the same for ourselves. Not only will we become more astute students of human nature, we'll become more sensitive and emotionally intelligent friends, partners, or parents.

In fact, the things we each push into our respective shadows are often not so different. *None of us* want to admit that we sometimes feel small and weak, unlovable, confused, lazy, selfish, lustful, jealous, mean, or cowardly. A great way to consider yours *and* the other person's shadow is to watch what feelings their behavior triggers in you.

For example, you might be having a conversation with the boastful intellectual from the earlier example. You share an idea that they laugh at and quickly denounce as "stupid." What's your response? If you're like most people, you may prickle with anger, embarrassment, or shame, and suddenly feel the need to defend yourself. Maybe you retort with something you think sounds extra intelligent to prove him wrong . . . or you simply laugh back and insult him directly.

What's happened is that his shadow has triggered yours. To have this reaction, somewhere inside you was the unwanted feeling of being stupid and inferior. If you have the presence of mind to remain conscious in such an interaction, however, you could pause and notice your own response and become curious about it. This person, in insulting you this way, has told you something very important about themselves, if you know how to listen.

Very astute and observant people know that what a person insults you with is often nothing more than the label they can't acknowledge they actually give themselves. If you realize this, you can keep your cool in such a conversation. If not, you may get hooked into a mutual ego-defense session— i.e., an argument—with the person, unknowingly accepting their invitation to play a particular shadow game with them.

The shadow expresses itself in people's motivations. The middle-aged man in the stereotypical story has suppressed out of consciousness his grief at the loss of his youth and sexual vigor. But it's out there for all to see in the form of his sexy new sports car. The next time you meet someone, quickly run through the following questions to help you see them on a deeper level:

- What is this person actively and consciously portraying to me right now?
- What might this person be unwilling to acknowledge about themselves?
- How might this unacknowledged part of themselves be unconsciously driving the behavior I see on the surface?
- How is this person making *me* feel right now? Do I feel like they are projecting onto me or triggering my own shadow?
- How can I communicate compassion and understanding for what's in their shadow, right now?

When you speak to someone, the shadow model helps you to speak to *all of them*, even the parts they don't show. It's a way of "reading between the lines" where people are concerned!

Our Inner Child Still Lives

Another related way of looking to people's deeper motivations is to recognize and acknowledge their "inner child." We can understand the inner child as that unconscious part of ourselves that represents the little children we once were.

After all, it's usually in childhood where we learn which parts of us are acceptable and which aren't, and hence it's the time we start to build up our shadow and shape our conscious personality. Doing "inner child work" sounds a little out there, but it's really not that different from gently acknowledging and embracing the shadow aspect.

If you were doing inner child work on your own or with a therapist, you might engage in a playful dialogue with your inner child, journal, draw and paint, and get into the mindset of a compassionate adult who then "re-parents" the younger version of yourself, giving yourself everything you needed back then but didn't receive.

How can we use the theory of the inner child to help us become better at reading people? In the same way we can learn to identify when someone is operating from their shadow, we can see if someone is motivated particularly from their inner child. If you're having an argument with a partner, and they're angry and defensive, you may suddenly see their behavior much more clearly if you understand it as a scared child essentially throwing a tantrum.

You've probably felt once or twice before as though you were dealing with a child who simply happened to be in the shape of a grown adult. If you notice someone suddenly acting with what seems like disproportionate emotion, pay attention. Feeling suddenly angry, hurt, defensive, or offended could be a clue that some nerve has been touched. The unconscious—whether that's the shadow or the inner child, or both—has been activated somehow.

A good indication that you're dealing with someone who is wholly identified with their child self is that you feel yourself positioned as a "parent." When we are adults, we are expected to take responsibility, show self-restraint, and behave with reason and respect for others. But a person in child mode may be (psychologically speaking) a child, which pushes you to respond as a parent would, i.e., with soothing, reprimanding, or taking responsibility for them.

Let's say you're asked to work with someone new at your job. This person flakes on meetings with you and then doesn't pitch in with their share of the work, leaving you to pick up the mess. When you confront them, they pout and deny it and sulk. You realize that this person is wholly identified with their inner child—who happens to be a naughty and rebellious child. Knowing this, you refrain from going into parent mode. You don't take on the responsibility of chastising them and trying to find a way to bribe them to do their job.

Perhaps this person learned early in life that this was the way to respond to authority, responsibilities, or things you didn't really want to do. By deliberately engaging with your colleague's adult aspect, however, you change the dynamic. You make it impossible for them to stay in child mode. What could have been a worse conflict ends up resolving eventually.

It's a subtle but powerful shift—we don't look only at the behavior in front of us, but *where the behavior is coming from and why*. True, we may not open up any additional avenues of choice by doing so, but we always enrich our understanding of the situation, which is intrinsically valuable.

One of psychology's lasting contributions to popular thought is the idea that we can interpret situations and events not just in terms of their practical features, but in terms of the people involved and their human needs and motivations. We'll look more closely at this theory in the following section.

The Motivation Factor—Pleasure or Pain

If you can zoom in and really grasp a person's true motivations, you can understand them so much better, perhaps even to the point of being able to predict how they might act in the future. Using this psychological approach gives you the opportunity to get into the perspective of other people, finding clarity on exactly what they *gain* by thinking and behaving as they do. With this knowledge, your interactions with people are instantly enriched.

Again, these intertwine neatly with emotions and values because they are often seeking the same ends. It's just another perspective on why someone will act the way they do and what we can understand of them from that.

Out of all the speculations about the sources of motivation, none is more famous than the *pleasure principle*. The reason it's so renowned is because it's also the easiest to understand. The pleasure principle was first raised in public consciousness by the father of psychoanalysis, Sigmund Freud, though researchers as far back as Aristotle in ancient Greece noted how easily we could be manipulated and motivated by pleasure and pain.

The pleasure principle asserts that the human mind does everything it can to seek out pleasure and avoid pain. It doesn't get simpler than that. In that simplicity, we find some of life's most universal and predictable motivators.

The pleasure principle is employed by our reptile brain, which can be said to house our natural drives and desires. It doesn't have any sense of restraint. It is primal and unfiltered. It goes after whatever it can to meet our body's urges for happiness and fulfillment. Anything that causes pleasure is felt by the brain the same way, whether it's a tasty meal or a drug. An apt comparison, in fact, is a drug addict who will stop at nothing to get another taste of narcotics.

There are a few rules that govern the pleasure principle, which also make us fairly predictable.

Every decision we make is based on gaining pleasure or avoiding pain. This is the common motivation for every person on earth. No matter what we do in the course of our day, it all gets down to the pleasure principle. You raid the refrigerator for snacks because you crave the taste and feel of certain food. You get a haircut because you think it will make you more attractive to someone else, which will make you happy, which is pleasure.

Conversely, you wear a protective mask while you're using a blowtorch because you want to avoid sparks flying into your face and eyes, because that will be painful. If you trace all of our decisions back, whether short term or long term, you'll find that they all stem from a small set of pleasures or pains.

People work harder to avoid pain than to get pleasure. While everyone wants pleasure as much as they can get it, their motivation to avoid pain is actually far stronger. The instinct to survive a threatening situation is more immediate than eating your favorite candy bar, for instance. So when faced with the prospect of pain, the brain will work harder than it would to gain access to pleasure.

For example, imagine you're standing in the middle of a desert road. In front of you is a treasure chest filled with money and outlandishly expensive jewelry that could set you up financially for the rest of your life. But there's also an out-of-control semi careening toward it. You're probably going to make the decision to jump away from the truck rather than grab the treasure chest, because your instinct to avoid pain—in this case, certain death—outweighed your desire to gain pleasure.

If you've hit rock bottom and faced a massive amount of pain or displeasure, then you simply must start acting to avoid that in the future. A wounded animal is more motivated than a slightly uncomfortable one.

Our perceptions of pleasure and pain are more powerful drivers than the actual things. When our brain is judging between what will be a pleasant or painful experience, it's working from scenarios that we *think* could result if we took a course of action. In other words, our *perceptions* of pleasure and pain are really what's driving the cart. And sometimes those perceptions can be flawed. In fact, they are mostly flawed, which explains our tendency to work against our own best interests.

I can think of no better example of this rule than jalapeño chapulines. They're a spicy, traditional Mexican snack that's tasty and low in carbs. By the way, "chapulines" means "grasshoppers." We're talking chili-flavored grasshoppers. The insects.

Now, you may have no firsthand knowledge of how grasshoppers taste. Maybe you've never tried them. But the *thought* of eating grasshoppers may give you pause. You imagine they'll be repellent to the tongue. You imagine if you take a bite of a grasshopper, you'll get grossed out. You might accidentally bite down on an internal grasshopper organ. The *perception* of eating a grasshopper is driving you quickly away from the act of eating one.

But the fact remains that *you haven't actually tried it yet.* You're working from your *idea* of the repulsion that eating a grasshopper will bring about. Somebody who's actually tried grasshopper-based cuisine may insist to you that they're really *good* when prepared properly. Still, you might not be able to get over your innate perception of what eating an insect would be like.

Pleasure and pain are changed by time. In general, we focus on the here and now: what can I get very soon that will bring me happiness? Also, what is coming up very soon that could be intensely painful that I'll have to avoid? When considering the attainment of comfort, we're more tuned into what might happen immediately. The pleasure and pain that might happen months or years from now don't really register with us—what's most important is whatever's right at our doorstep. Of course, this is another way in which our perceptions are flawed and why we procrastinate so frequently, for example.

Suppose a smoker needs a cigarette. It's the main focus of their current situation. It brings them a certain relief or pleasure. And in about fifteen minutes, they'll be on break so they can enjoy that cigarette. It's the focus of their daily ritual. They're *not* thinking how smoking a cigarette every time they "need" one could cause painful health problems down the road. That's a distant reality that's not driving them at all. Right now, they need a smoke because they crave one, and they might get a headache immediately if they don't get one.

Emotion beats logic. When it comes to the pleasure principle, your feelings tend to overshadow rational thought. You might know that doing something will be good or bad for you. You'll understand all the reasons why it will be good or bad. You'll get all that. But if your illogical id is so intent on satisfying a certain craving, then it's probably going to win out. And if your id drives you to think that doing something useful will cause too much stress or temporary dissatisfaction, it's going to win there too.

Going back to our smoker, without a doubt they know why cigarettes are bad for one's health. They've read those warnings on the packages. Maybe in school they saw a picture of a corroded lung that resulted from years of smoking. They *know* all the risks they're about to court. But there's that pack right in front of them. And all reason be damned, they're going to have that cigarette. Their emotions oriented toward pleasure win out.

Survival overrides everything. When our survival instinct gets activated, everything else in our psychological and emotional makeup turns off. If a life-threatening situation (or a *perceived* life-threatening situation) arises in our existence, the brain closes down everything else and turns us into a machine whose thoughts and actions are all oriented toward the will to survive.

This shouldn't be surprising when it comes to avoiding painful outcomes. Of *course* you're going to try to jump away from that oncoming semi truck; if you don't, you won't survive. Your system won't let you make that choice—it's going to do everything it can to get you the hell out of the way of that truck.

However, survival can *also* come into play when we're seeking pleasure—even if it means we might slip into harm's way. The most obvious example of this is food. Say you're at a bar and somebody orders a giant plate of nachos loaded with cheese, sour cream, fatty meat, and a bunch of other things that might not be the best dietary choices for you. You *might* be able to resist it. Some people can. But you might not. In fact, you could find yourself eating half the plate before you even know what you've done.

Why? Because you need food to survive. And your brain is telling you there's food in the vicinity, so perhaps you should eat it. Never mind that it's not the best kind of food, nutritionally speaking, that you could opt for at the moment. Your survival instinct is telling you it's time to have those nachos. Your life depends on it.

The pleasure principle is related to an idea that comes from economics and the attempt to predict markets and human buying behavior: the *rational choice theory*, embodied by the jokingly named *Homo economicus*. This states that all of our choices and decisions spring entirely from self-interest and the desire to bring as much pleasure to our lives as possible. It may not always hold up (otherwise market and stock prices would be one hundred percent predictable), but it provides more support for the simple nature of many of our motivations.

The next time you meet someone new or are trying to get a read on someone, consider looking at their actions in terms of the motivation of pleasure or pain. Ask yourself what good thing they gain by behaving as they do, or what bad thing they avoid—or both.

For example, if you have a tired five-year-old who doesn't want to clean up their room, you might consider pleasure and pain and ask how they perceive your request: probably as painful! When you realize that they are simply behaving to avoid pain and maximize their own pleasure, you can reframe your request. If you can turn tidying up into a fun game, or if you can link tidying up to the anticipation of a reward, you've communicated effectively and gotten the result you want.

Of course, you're probably wondering if this theory always applies—the answer is no. People are able to exercise discipline, restraint, and self-control, and they are able to genuinely desire and derive pleasure from doing things that only pay off in the future, or only help others and not themselves. Though the pleasure/pain principle may work well with dog training, you probably like to think of yourself as a little more complex, morally speaking.

For example, there are countless stories of prisoners held in concentration camps during the holocaust, who were starving to death and yet chose to share what little food they had with those around them. Naturally, a human being is driven to act by many more things than simple pleasure seeking or pain avoidance. This is why learning to read people requires us to consider so many different models and theories—none of them are sufficient on their own.

In the following section, we'll look at another needs-based theory that can help us better make sense of people who act outside of the normal pleasure/pain dynamics, and why.

The Pyramid of Needs

Maslow's hierarchy of needs is one of the most famous models in the history of psychology. It employs a pyramid to show how certain human "needs"—like food, sleep, and warmth—are necessary to resolve before more aspirational needs like love, accomplishment, and vocation. Maslow's pyramid can be viewed as a visual example of how motivation changes and increases after we get what we need at each stage in our lives, which typically coincides with where we are on the hierarchy itself.

When psychology professor Abraham Maslow came along in the 1940s, his theory boiled everything down to one revolutionary idea: human beings are a product of a set of basic human needs, the deprivation of which is the primary cause of most psychological problems. Fulfilling these needs is what drives us on a daily basis.

The hierarchy, now named for him, maps out basic human needs and desires and how they evolve throughout life. It functions like a ladder—if you aren't able to satisfy your more basic foundational human needs and desires, it is extremely difficult to move forward without stress and dissatisfaction in life. It means your motivations change depending on where you are in the hierarchy.

To illustrate, let's take a look at how our needs and associated motivations change from infancy to adulthood. As infants, we don't feel any need for a career or life satisfaction. We simply need to rest, be fed, and have shelter over our heads. Feeding and survival are our only real needs and desires (as parents of newborns will tell you).

As we grow from infants into teenagers, simply staying alive and healthy doesn't bring satisfaction. We hunger for interpersonal relationships and friendships. What drives us is to find a feeling of belonging and community. Then, as we mature into young adults, simply having a great group of friends is no longer enough to satisfy us. It feels empty, actually, without an overall sense of purpose.

If, as young adults, we are fortunate enough to be able to provide financial security and stability for ourselves and our families, then our desires and needs can turn outward rather than inward. It's the same reason that people like Warren Buffett and Bill Gates start participating in philanthropy to make as big an impact as they can on the world.

The stages of Maslow's hierarchy of needs determine exactly what you're motivated by depending on where you are in the hierarchy.

The first stage is physiological fulfillment. This is easily seen in the daily life of an infant. All that matters to them is that their basic needs for survival are met (i.e., food, water, and shelter). Without security in these aspects, it is difficult for anyone to focus on satisfaction in anything else—it would actually be harmful to them to seek other forms of satisfaction. So this is the baseline level of fulfillment that must first be met.

The second stage is safety. If someone's belly is full, they have clothes on their back, and they have a roof over their head, they need to find a way to ensure that those things keep on coming. They need to have a secure source of income or resources to increase the certainty and longevity of their safety. The first two stages are designed to ensure overall survival. Unfortunately, many people never make it out of these first two stages due to unfortunate circumstances, and you can plainly see why they aren't concerned with fulfilling their potential.

The third stage is love and belonging. Now that your survival is ensured, you'll find that it is relatively empty without sharing it with people you care about. Humans are social creatures, and case studies have shown that living in isolation will literally cause insanity and mental instability, no matter how well fed or secure you are. This includes relationships with your friends and family and socializing enough so you don't feel that you are failing in your social life.

Of course, this stage is a major sticking point for many people—they are unable to be fulfilled or focus on higher desires because they lack the relationships that create a healthy lifestyle. Isn't it easy to imagine someone who is stuck at a low level of happiness because they don't have any friends?

The fourth stage is self-esteem. You can have relationships, but are they healthy ones that make you feel confident and supported?

This stage is all about how your interactions with others impact your relationship with yourself. This is a very interesting level of maturity in terms of needs because it boils down to self-acceptance. You know you have a healthy level of self-esteem when you can accept yourself even if you are misunderstood or outright disliked by others. For you to get to this stage and have a healthy level of self-esteem, you have to have accumulated certain achievements or earned the respect of others. There is a strong interplay between how you get along with others and help others and how you feel about yourself.

The final stage is self-actualization. The highest level of Maslow's hierarchy is self-actualization. This is when you are able to live for something higher than yourself and your needs. You feel that you need to connect with principles that require you to step beyond what is convenient and what is comfortable. This is the plane of morality, creativity, spontaneity, lack of prejudice, and acceptance of reality.

Self-actualization is placed at the top of the pyramid because this is the highest (and last) need people have. All the lower levels have to be met first before a person can reach this last level. You know you are working with somebody who operates at a truly high level when they do not focus so much on what is important to them, their self-esteem, or how other people perceive them. This is the stage people are at when they say they want to find their calling and purpose in life.

Maslow's theory may not accurately describe all of our daily desires, but it does provide an inventory for the broad strokes of what we want in life. We can observe people to understand which stage of life they are in, what is currently important to them, and what they require to get to the next level in the hierarchy.

Consider a counselor who works at a women's shelter. She can use the pyramid of needs to help her decide how to approach and communicate with the women who come there for help. She knows that when a woman first turns up, she is primarily concerned with her *physical* safety. If she is fleeing domestic violence, trying to secure funds, or is worried about the well-being of her children, she's not going to be in a position to sit down and work through a cheesy self-love workbook with the counselor. At the same time, a woman who has been at the shelter for a few months has her physical needs largely fulfilled, but may be in the mindset of needing to feel companionship and belonging. The counselor knows that she needs to befriend and support such a woman.

It would be utterly useless to try to talk to either of these women about high-level concepts like compassionately forgiving your abuser or going on to make meaning of your story. On the other hand, a woman who survived domestic abuse and was recovering well might have needs higher up on the hierarchy, and will seek more for herself. A good counselor would use this knowledge to frame how she spoke to each one, and tailor her advice and support to match each woman's deeper motivation. Such a counselor would no doubt be described as a person who understood others.

But let's say the counselor encounters a woman one day who is beaten black and blue by her partner, but nevertheless denies that she's being abused, and simply changes the topic when anyone mentions it. What's going on here? Our next section explores one key way in which people seek pleasure, avoid pain, and try to address their needs— that is, through defense mechanisms.

Defense of the Ego

Protecting yourself from others is a frequent reason for our behaviors, and we are highly motivated to shield the ego for many reasons. The ego's instinct to protect itself can be reality-bending and can cause mass intellectual dishonesty and self-deception. As such, this is another highly predictable indicator we can use to analyze people's behavior.

Someone who's underperforming at work might feel the need to protect their perceived skills and talent by deflecting responsibility to: "The boss has always had it in for me. And who trained me? Him! It's all his fault one way or another." Someone who trips and falls yet fancies themselves graceful will blame the fact that it rained six days ago, their shoes have no grip, and *who put that rock there, anyway*? Someone who fails to make the school basketball team will grumble that the coach hated them, they weren't used to that particular style of play, and they didn't *really* want to make the team, anyway.

This is what it sounds like when the ego steps in to protect itself. There's so much justification and deflecting going on that it's difficult to know what is real and what is not.

This all stems from the universal truth that nobody likes to be wrong or to fail. It's embarrassing and confirms all of our worst anxieties about ourselves. Instead of accepting being wrong as a teachable moment or lesson, our first instinct is to run from our shame and cower in the corner. This is the same reason we will persist in an argument to the death, even if we know we are one hundred percent wrong. If the ego had a physical manifestation, it would be sizable, sensitive, and heavily armored (to the point of going on the offensive)— essentially a giant porcupine.

When the ego senses danger, it has no interest or time to consider the facts. Instead, it seeks to alleviate discomfort in the quickest way possible. And that means you lie to yourself so you can keep the ego safe and sound.

We try to cover up the truth, deflect attention from it, or develop an alternative version that makes the actual truth seem less hurtful. And it's right in that moment that intellectual dishonesty is born. Are any of those convoluted theories likely to withstand any amount of scrutiny? Probably not, but the problem is that the ego doesn't allow for acknowledgment and analysis of what really happened. It blinds you.

Let's be clear: these aren't lies that you dream up or concoct in advance. You do not *intend* to lie to yourself. You don't even *feel* they're lies. You may not even know you're doing it, as sometimes these defense mechanisms can occur unconsciously. They're not explicitly intellectually dishonest because you *want* to delude yourself. Rather, they're automatic strategies that the constantly neurotic ego puts into action because it's terrified of looking foolish or wrong. Unfortunately, that's the worst zone to be in, as it means *you don't know what you don't know*.

Over time, these ego-driven errors in thinking inform your entire belief system and give you rationalized justifications for almost everything. You never make any sports team because the coaches always hate you, and you keep failing the driving test because your hand-eye coordination is *uniquely special.*

These lies become your entire reality, and you rely on them to get yourself through problematic situations or to dismiss efforts to find the truth. We're not talking about just giving excuses for why you aren't a violin virtuoso; this manner of thinking can become the factors that drive your decisions, thinking, and evaluations of anything and anyone.

So if you're struggling to understand someone who doesn't appear to be able to utter the words "I'm wrong," now you know exactly what's going on in their head. They may not know, but at least you are able to analyze them more deeply.

Let's take Fred. Fred was an ardent fan of a pop star his whole life. He grew up listening to his music and formed a lot of his identity around his admiration for him. We're talking an entire bedroom wall filled with posters of this star and outfits that were replicas of this star's clothes hanging in his closet.

Late in his career, this pop star was put on trial for a serious crime. Fred steadfastly stood by his pop star idol, even as lurid details of his case were reported by courtroom reporters to the press. "Nobody I admire this way would ever be guilty of this," Fred said. "It's all just a conspiracy put together by the people who resent him for whatever reason."

The pop star was ultimately found guilty and sentenced to multiple years in prison. Fred had shown up outside the courthouse bearing a sign that protested his star's innocence. Even as compelling evidence was eventually released to the press, Fred maintained that the pop star was absolutely innocent, dismissing all of the victims' claims by protesting that they were "jealous" and "just trying to get into the spotlight themselves."

Why would Fred continue to insist, against all reasonable and provable evidence, that his idol was innocent? Because his ego was so wrapped up in his worship of the pop star that it was predisposed to consider him blameless. For him to believe the truth would have meant a devastating blow to almost everything he believed in (*I worship a criminal? What does that say about me?),* and the ego wasn't going to let that happen for a minute—even if it meant making him deny compelling and unshakable proof that the star was guilty.

In your pursuit of truth and clear thought, your ego will rear its ugly head like the enraged porcupine. It has set up a series of tactical barriers to keep you from learning something that might upset your belief system, and it is only after you can rein in your ego that you are open to learning. After all, you can't defend yourself and listen at the same time.

Defense mechanisms are the specific ways we protect our ego, pride, and self-esteem. These methods keep us whole when times are tough. The origin of the term comes from Sigmund Freud.

These so-called defense mechanisms are also a powerful predictor of behavior and will give you a deep insight into why people do what they do. Defense mechanisms can take many varied and colorful forms, but there are a few common patterns that you'll see in others (and hopefully yourself!). These psychological shields rear up when the ego senses something it doesn't agree with, can't face, or wishes wasn't true.

Loss, rejection, uncertainty, discomfort, humiliation, loneliness, failure, panic . . . all of these can be defended against using certain mental tricks. These mechanisms are there to protect us from experiencing negative emotions. They work in the moment, but in the long run, they are ineffective since they rob us of the opportunity to face, accept, and digest inevitably negative emotions as they crop up.

Naturally, if you can observe somebody using a defense mechanism, you can instantly infer a lot about them and their world, particularly about the things they find themselves unable to deal with. This in turn tells you a lot about how they see themselves, their strengths and weaknesses, and what they value. Let's look at some defense mechanisms with concrete examples. You just might recognize these two defense mechanisms put forth by his daughter, Anna Freud: denial and rationalization.

Denial is one of the most classic defense mechanisms because it is easy to use. Suppose you discovered that you were performing poorly at your job. "No, I don't believe that report ranking all the employees. There's no way I can be last. Not in this world. The computer added up the scores incorrectly."

What is true is simply claimed to be false, as if that makes everything go away. You are acting as if a negative fact doesn't exist. Sometimes we don't realize when we do this, especially in situations that are so dire they actually appear fantastical to us.

All you have to do is say "no" often enough and you might begin to believe yourself, and that's where the appeal of denial lies. You are actually changing your reality, where other defense mechanisms merely spin it to be more acceptable. This is actually the most dangerous defense mechanism, because even if there is a dire problem, it is ignored and never fixed. If someone continued to persist in the belief they were an excellent driver, despite a string of accidents in the past year, it's unlikely they would ever seek to practice their driving skills.

Rationalization is when you explain away something negative.

It is the art of making excuses. The bad behavior or fact still remains, but it is turned into something unavoidable because of circumstances out of your control. The bottom line is that anything negative is not your fault and you shouldn't be held accountable for it. It's never a besmirching of your abilities. It's extremely convenient, and you are only limited by your imagination.

Building on the same prior example of poor job performance, this is easily explained away by the following: your boss secretly hating you, your coworkers plotting against you, the computer being biased against your soft skills, unpredictable traffic affecting your commute, and having two jobs at once. These flimsy excuses are what your ego needs to protect itself.

Rationalization is the embodiment of the *sour grapes fable.* A fox wanted to reach some grapes at the top of a bush, but he couldn't leap high enough. To make himself feel better about his lack of leaping ability, and to comfort himself about his lack of grapes, he told himself the grapes looked sour, anyway, so he wasn't missing out on anything. He was still hungry, but he'd rather be hungry than admit his failure.

Rationalization can also help us feel at peace with poor decisions we've made, with phrases such as, "It was going to happen at some point, anyway." Rationalization ensures you never have to face failure, rejection, or negativity. It's always someone else's fault!

While comforting, where do reality and truth go amidst all of this? Out the window, mostly. Intellectual honesty requires you to first defeat your natural tendencies to be dishonest. Thoughts dictated by self-protection don't overlap with clear, objective thoughts.

Closely associated is **repression**. Whereas in denial the reality is refused or downright rejected, repression is where a person pushes the thought or feeling so far out of consciousness, they "forget" it. It's as though the threatening emotion never existed in the first place. An example might be a child who experiences abuse. Because it is so painful, and because they had no way of helping themselves, they might push the memory so far away that they never have to deal with it.

Sometimes, the overpowering emotion is unwelcome, but what is really unacceptable to the ego is *where* it comes from. In such a case, **displacement** might occur as a protection against unpleasant truths. A woman might work at a job she hates but cannot realistically leave. Simply, she cannot express or even acknowledge that she resents her job because this draws a threatening attention to her financial bind.

What she might do, though, is take that resentment and put it elsewhere. She might come home every day and kick the dog or yell at her children, convinced that they are the ones making her angry. It is easier and less risky to confront her feelings of anger when they are directed to her pets or children.

Projection is a defense mechanism that can cause considerable damage and chaos if not understood for what it is. In this case, we place unwanted and unclaimed feelings onto someone or something else rather than seeing that they are a part of ourselves. We do not recognize our own "dark side" and project it onto others, blaming them for our shortcomings or seeing our flaws in their actions.

An example is a man who is cheating on his wife. He finds his own behavior unacceptable, but rather than allow himself to condemn his own actions, he projects that shame onto his (bewildered) partner and is suddenly suspicious of her behavior, accusing *her* of keeping something from *him*.

The example of a blatantly homophobic man who is revealed to later be gay is so common by now it's almost comical. **_Reaction formation_** just might be behind it. Whereas denial simply says, "This isn't happening," reaction formation goes a step further and claims, "Not only is that not happening, but the exact opposite is the case. Look!"

A woman might be terrified of her new cancer diagnosis and, rather than admit her fear, puts on a show to everyone of being courageous, preaching to others about how death is nothing to fear.

In times of extreme emotional distress, you might find yourself **_regressing_** to a simpler time (i.e., childhood). When you were young, life was easier and less demanding— to cope with threatening emotions, many of us return there, acting "childish" as a way to cope. A man might be facing some legal troubles over misfiled taxes. Rather than face the situation, he gets into a screaming match with his accountant, banging his fists on the table in a "tantrum" and then pouting when people try to reason with him.

Finally, we come to **sublimation.** In the same way that projection and displacement take the negative emotions and place them elsewhere, sublimation takes that emotion and channels it through a different, more acceptable outlet. A single man might find the loneliness at home unbearable and channels that unmet need into doing charity work four nights a week. A woman may receive some bad news, but rather than get upset, she goes home and proceeds to do a massive spring clean of her home. A person might routinely turn panic and anxiety into a dedication to prayer, and so on.

Defense of the ego is a nasty habit, but it's easy to recognize when you know of its insidious presence. Sometimes we can't help it; we're all human. But we can use this to our advantage by using it as a clear quantity to analyze people with.

Takeaways

- We've talked about analyzing and predicting behavior based on people's emotions and values, but what about motivation? It turns out there are a few prominent and fairly universal models of motivation that can give you a helpful framework to understand people with. When you can pinpoint what people are motivated by, you can see how everything leads back to it either directly or indirectly.

- Any discussion on motivation must begin with the pleasure principle, which generally states that we move toward pleasure and move away from pain. If you think about it, this is omnipresent in our daily lives in both minuscule and huge ways. As such, this actually makes people more predictable to understand. What is the pleasure people are seeking, and what is the pain they are avoiding? It's always there in some way.

- Next, we move to the pyramid of needs, otherwise known as Abraham Maslow's hierarchy of needs. It states that we are all seeking various types of needs in various points in our lives; when you can observe which level other people are in, you can understand what they are seeking out and motivated by. The levels of the hierarchy are as follows: physiological fulfillment, safety, love and belonging, self-esteem, and self-actualization. Of course, this model, as well as the next one, also functions based on the pleasure principle.

- Finally, we come to defense of the ego. This is one of our most powerful motivators, but it is mostly unconscious. Simply put, we act to guard our ego from anything that would make us feel psychologically *less*. In doing so, it is so powerful that it allows us to bend reality and lie to ourselves and others—all outside of our conscious awareness. Defense mechanisms are the ways that we avoid responsibility and negative feelings, and they include denial, rationalization, projection, sublimation, regression, displacement, repression, and reaction formation, to name a few. When you know the ego is in play, it often takes front stage over other motivations.

Chapter 2. The Body, the Face, and Clusters

The idea that people cannot help but reveal their true intentions and feelings one way or another is an appealing one. People can *say* whatever they like, but it's always been understood that "actions speak louder than words" and that people's facial expressions or body language can inadvertently reveal their deepest selves. We are in effect communicating all the time, sending out information about our intentions and feelings—but only a small fraction of this is verbal.

Observing people's actions and behavior in real time is what we most commonly understand to be analyzing people. It might seem natural to look to people's physical bodies in space to intuit what's going on in their heads, and there's plenty of scientific evidence to support these claims. Physical appearance can tell you a lot about a person's feelings, motivations, and fears, even if they're actively trying to conceal these. In other words, the body doesn't lie!

Nevertheless, this approach to understanding people's motivations is not foolproof. When we're interacting with others and trying to understand what makes them tick, it's important to be cautious in making assumptions. We're all individuals, and context is very important. Though we can use various methods to read facial expressions and body language, it pays to remember that no single piece of information is enough to "prove" anything, and that the art of reading people this way comes down to taking a holistic view of the full scenario as it unfolds in front of you.

Look at my Face

Let's begin with Haggard and Isaacs in the 1960s. They filmed couples' faces during therapy and noticed little expressions that could only be caught when the film was slowed down. Later on, Paul Ekman expanded on his own theory on *microexpressions* and published a book, *Telling Lies*.

We all know how to read *macro*expressions—those facial movements that last up to four seconds in duration—but there are quicker, more fleeting expressions that are so fast, they could easily be missed by the untrained eye. According to Ekman, facial expressions are actually physiological reactions. These expressions occur even when you're not around anyone who could see them. He found that across cultures, people used microexpressions to display their emotions on their faces in very predictable ways—even when they were attempting to conceal them or even when they themselves were unaware of the emotion.

His research led him to believe that microexpressions are spontaneous, tiny contractions of certain muscle groups that are predictably related to emotions and are the same in all people, regardless of upbringing, background, or cultural expectation. They can be as quick as one-thirtieth of a second long. But catching them and understanding what they mean is a way to cut through what is merely said to get to the deeper truth of what people feel and believe. Macroexpressions can be, to some extent, forced or exaggerated, but microexpressions are understood to be more genuine and difficult to fake or else suggestive of concealed or rapidly changing emotions.

Within the brain, there are two neural pathways related to facial expressions. The first is the *pyramidal tract*, responsible for voluntary expressions (i.e., most macroexpressions), and the *extrapyramidal tract*, responsible for involuntary emotional facial expressions (i.e., microexpressions). Researchers have discovered that individuals who experience intense emotional situations but also external pressure to control or hide that expression will show activity in *both* these brain pathways. This suggests that they're working against one another, with the more conscious and voluntary expressions dominating the involuntary ones. Nevertheless, some tiny expressions of the real emotion may "leak" out—this is what you're looking for when you attempt to read a person in this way.

So just exactly how does one learn to read these expressions? Can you really decode a person's deepest feelings just by looking at a twitch of their nose or a wrinkle in their brow?

According to Ekman, there are six universal human emotions, all with corresponding minuscule facial expressions. Happiness is seen in lifted cheeks, with the corners of the mouth raised up and back. Wrinkles appear under the eyes, between the upper lip and nose, and in the outside corner of the eyes. In other words, the movements we're all familiar with in an ordinary smile are there on a micro level too.

Microexpressions suggesting sadness are also what you'd expect. The outer corner of the eyes droops down, along with the corners of the lips. The lower lip may even tremble. Eyebrows may form a telltale triangle shape. For the emotion of disgust, the upper lip lifts and may be accompanied by wrinkles above it and wrinkles on the forehead. The eyes may narrow slightly as the cheeks are raised.

For anger, eyebrows lower and tense up, often at a downward angle. Eyes tighten, too, and the lips may be pursed or held stiffly open. The eyes are staring and piercing. Fear, on the other hand, entails similar contractions but upward. Whether open or closed, the mouth is tense, and both upper and lower eyelids are lifted. Finally, surprise or shock will show itself in elevated brows—rounded rather than triangular, like with sadness. The upper eyelids lift up and the lower eyelids stretch downward, opening the eyes wide. Sometimes, the jaw can hang loosely open.

As you can see, microexpressions are not very different from macroexpressions in the muscles that are involved; the main difference is in their speed. Ekman demonstrated, however, that these quick flashes of muscle contraction are so fast that people miss them: ninety-nine percent of people were unable to perceive them. Nevertheless, he also claims that people can be trained to look for microexpressions and in particular learn to detect liars, a classic example of saying one thing and feeling another.

Ekman claims to be able to teach his technique within thirty-two hours, but for those of us who are curious about using the principles in our own lives, it's easy to start. Firstly, look for discrepancies between what is said and what is actually demonstrated through facial expressions. For example, someone might be assuring you verbally and making promises but showing quick expressions of fear that betray their real position.

Other classic indicators that you are being lied to include lifting the shoulders slightly while someone is vehemently confirming the truth of what they're saying. Scratching the nose, moving the head to the side, avoiding eye contact, uncertainty in speaking, and general fidgeting also indicate someone's internal reality is not exactly lining up with the external—i.e., they might be lying.

Again, it's worth mentioning here that this is not a foolproof method and that research has mostly failed to find a strong relationship between body language, facial expression, and deceitfulness. No single gesture alone indicates anything. Many psychologists have since pointed out that discrepancies in microexpressions can actually indicate discomfort, nervousness, stress, or tension, without deception being involved.

Nevertheless, when used as a tool along with other tools, and when taken in context, microexpression analysis can be powerful. Granted, you'll need to stare quite intently at the person and observe them in a way that's uncomfortable and too obvious for normal social situations. You'll also have to weed out tons of irrelevant data and decide what gestures count as "noise" or meaningless idiosyncrasies.

At any rate, people who lack the required training have been shown to be astoundingly bad at spotting liars—despite feeling as though their gut intuitions about others' deceit is reliable. This means that even a slight increase in accuracy you might gain from understanding and implementing the microexpression theory may make all the difference. A microexpression may be small, but it's still a data point.

All this talk of unmasking liars may make this technique seem rather combative and underhanded, but Ekman is careful to point out that "lies" and "deceit," as he frames them, can also indicate the hiding of an emotion and not necessarily any malicious intent. There is certainly an allure in playing detective and uncovering people's secret feelings, but in reality, the use of microexpression analysis is a bit like CSI: it always looks a bit more impressive on TV than it is in real life. Furthermore, the goal in developing the skill of microexpression analysis is not to play "gotcha!" to our friends and colleagues, but rather to enhance our own empathy and emotional intelligence and foster a richer understanding of the people around us.

If you're not convinced about using microexpressions to detect deception, another perspective is not to look for lies or classify expressions according to their duration, but rather to look at what an expression typically conveys. Then, depending on context and how the expression compares to what's said *verbally*, you can come to your own conclusions.

Nervousness is typically behind things like tightening the lips or twitching the corners of the mouth very quickly toward the ear and back. Quivering lips or chin, a furrowed brow, narrowed eyes, and pulled-in lips may also indicate the person is feeling tense. If a person you know is normally calm and composed but you suddenly notice plenty of these little signs while they tell you a tale you don't quite believe, you might infer that, for some reason, they're nervous about telling it to you. Whether this is because they're lying or because their story is simply uncomfortable to tell—only you can decide from context.

A person feeling dislike or disagreement might purse their lips tightly, roll their eyes, flutter their eyelids briefly, or crinkle their nose. They may also squint a little or narrow their eyes like a cartoon villain staring down the hero, close their eyes, or "sneer" a little in a slight expression of disdain. If a person opens the Christmas present you gave them and immediately proceeds to do all of the above, you might want to assume they don't really like their gift, despite what they say to the contrary.

Those dealing with stress may find tiny ways to release that stress, giving themselves away even though for the most part they appear quite calm. Uncontrollable, fast blinking and making repetitive motions like twitching the cheek, biting the tongue, or touching parts of the face with their fingers can all indicate someone who's finding a particular situation stressful. This might make sense when someone's in a job interview or being questioned in connection with a crime but may be more noteworthy if you spot it in seemingly calm situations. This discrepancy gives you a clue that all might not be as it appears.

Pay attention also to asymmetry in facial expressions. Natural, spontaneous, and genuine expressions of emotion tend to be symmetrical. Forced, fake, or conflicting expressions tend not to be. And again, try to interpret what you see in context, and consider the whole person, including other body language.

Remember that analyzing facial expressions is a powerful method of understanding others that's more than "skin-deep," but it's not foolproof. Every observation you make is simply a data point and doesn't prove anything either way. The skill comes in gathering as much data as you can and interpreting the whole, emerging pattern before you, rather than just one or two signs. For this reason, it's best to use what you know about microexpressions as a supplement to other methods and tools.

Body Talk

Body language, for instance, may be just as powerful a language to learn to read and comprehend as facial expressions. After all, the face is simply a part of the body. Why focus on just one part when people's postures and general movements can speak just as eloquently? Ex-FBI agent Joe Navarro is generally considered an authority in this field and has used his experience to teach others about the wealth of information people share without ever opening their mouths (i.e., what he calls "nonverbal communication").

Originally from Cuba and having to learn English after moving to the U.S. when he was eight years old, Navarro quickly came to appreciate how the human body was "a kind of billboard that advertised what a person was thinking." During his career he spoke at length about learning to spot people's "tells"—those little movements that suggest that someone is uncomfortable, hostile, relaxed, or fearful.

As with facial expressions, these tells may hint at deceit or lies but primarily indicate that someone is uncomfortable or that there is a discrepancy between what's felt and what's expressed. Armed with an understanding of how body language works, we can not only open up new channels on which to communicate with others, but pay attention to our own bodies and the messages we may be unwittingly sending to others.

Firstly, it's important to understand that nonverbal communication is inbuilt, biological, and the result of evolution. Our emotional responses to certain things are lightning-fast, and they happen spontaneously, whether we want them to or not. Importantly, they express themselves physically in the way we hold and move our bodies in space, potentially resulting in the transmission of thousands of nonverbal messages.

It's the more primitive, emotional, and perhaps honest part of our brain, the limbic brain, that's responsible for these automatic responses. While the prefrontal cortex (the more intellectual and abstract part) is a little removed from the body, and more under conscious control, it's also the part that's capable of lying. But even though a person can say one thing, their bodies will always speak the truth. If you can tune into the gestures, movements, postures, patterns of touching, and even the clothing a person wears, you give yourself a more direct channel into what they *really* think and feel. Navarro claims that the majority of communication is nonverbal anyway—meaning you're actively missing out on the bulk of the message by *not* considering body language.

Consider that communication started out nonverbally. In our earliest histories, before the development of language, humankind most likely communicated by gestures, simple sounds, and facial expressions. In fact, from the moment a baby is born it instinctively makes faces to communicate that it's cold, hungry, or frightened. We never need to be taught how to read basic gestures or understand tones of voice—this is because nonverbal communication was our first communication and may still be our preferred form.

Think of all the ways you already take nonverbal communication for granted—in the way you show love or demonstrate your anger. Even if you aren't aware of it, we are all still processing vast amounts of information on nonverbal channels. Learn how to read this information and you can determine if someone is trying to deceive you or perhaps if someone is trying to conceal their feelings and true intentions from you.

You've probably heard of the "fight-or-flight" response before, but there's a third possibility: freeze. What's more, these responses to danger may be quite subtle, but nevertheless, they speak to discomfort and fear. Our ancestors might have shown fight-or-flight when running from predators or enemy tribes, but those instincts might have followed us into the boardroom or classroom.

The limbic brain is again responsible for these fear responses. Someone who is asked a difficult question or put on the spot may look like a deer caught in headlights. They may lock their legs around a chair and stay fixed tight in that position (this is the freeze response). Another possibility is physically moving the body away from what is perceived as threatening. A person may put an object on their lap or position their limbs toward the exit (the flight response). Finally, a third person may "fight." This aggressive response to fear can show itself in picking arguments, verbally "sparring," or adopting threatening gestures.

In fact, the more competent you become at reading nonverbal signals, the more you may come to appreciate how fundamentally *physical* they are and how much they speak to our shared evolutionary history. In the past we might have literally fended off an attack with certain gestures or indeed set out to attack another with very obvious movements and expressions. These days, our world is very abstract and the things that threaten us are more verbal and conceptual—but the old machinery for expression, fear, aggression, curiosity, etc. is all still there, only perhaps expressed a little more subtly.

Let's consider what are called "pacifying behaviors." These can offer a key insight into someone who is feeling stressed, unsure, or threatened. Essentially, a pacifying behavior is what it sounds like— the (unconscious) attempt to self-soothe in the face of some perceived threat. When we feel stressed, our limbic brain may compel us to make little gestures designed to calm us: touching the forehead, rubbing the neck, fiddling with hair, or wringing the hands are all behaviors intended to soothe stress.

The neck is a vulnerable area of the body, but one that is relatively exposed. Consider how aggressive people "go for the jugular" and you understand how the throat and neck can be unconsciously felt to be an area open for fatal attack. It makes sense then that someone unconsciously covering or stroking this area is expressing their struggle, emotional discomfort, or insecurity. Men may use this gesture more often than women; men may fidget with their ties or squeeze the top of the neck, while women may put the fingers to the suprasternal notch (the indent between the collarbones) or play nervously with a necklace.

Pay attention to this behavior and you'll notice how it reveals someone's fears and insecurities in real-time. Someone might say something a little aggressive and another person responds by leaning back slightly, crossing the arms, and putting one hand up to the throat. Notice this in real-time and you can infer that this particular statement has aroused some fear and uncertainty.

Similarly, rubbing or touching the forehead or temples can signal emotional distress or overwhelm. A quick tap with the fingers may reveal a momentary feeling of stress, whereas a prolonged cradling of the head in both hands can spell extreme distress. In fact, you can consider any cradling, stroking, or rubbing movement as the physical clue of a person's need to self-pacify. This could mean touching cheeks when the person feels nervous or frightened, rubbing or licking the lips, massaging the earlobes, or running the fingers through the hair or beard.

Pacifying behaviors are not just things liked stroking or rubbing, though. Puffing out the cheeks and exhaling loudly is also a gesture that releases considerable stress. Have you ever noticed how many people will do this after hearing bad news or narrowly escaping an accident? An unexpected stress release response is yawning—rather than indicating boredom, the body's sudden attempt to draw in more oxygen during stressful times is even seen in other animals. "Leg cleansing" is another, and it entails wiping down the legs as though to wash them or brush off dust. This can be missed if it's hidden under a table, but if you can notice it, it is a strong indication of an attempt to self-soothe during stressful moments.

"Ventilating" is another behavior you may not pay much attention to. Notice someone pulling their shirt collar away from their neck or tossing the hair away from the shoulders as though to cool off. They're likely experiencing discomfort or tension. Though this might be literally because of an uncomfortable environment, it's more likely a response to inner tension and stress that needs "cooling off."

One of the most obvious forms of pacifying behavior looks exactly like what a mother might do to a young child to soothe them: cradling and hugging one's own body or rubbing the shoulders as though to ward off a chill all suggest a person who feels under threat, worried, or overwhelmed—these gestures are an unconscious way to protect the body.

This is an important underlying principle across all of body language theory: that limbs and gestures may signal unconscious attempts to protect and defend the body. When you consider that the torso contains all the body's vital organs, you can understand why the limbic brain has reflex responses to shield this area when threats are perceived—even emotional threats.

Someone who is highly unresponsive to a request or who feels attacked or criticized may cross their arms as if to say, "Back off." Raising the arms to the chest during an argument is a classic blocking gesture, almost as if the words being exchanged were literally thrown, causing an unconscious reflex to fend them off. On a similar note, slumping, loose arms can indicate defeat, disappointment, or despair. It's as though the body is physically broadcasting the nonphysical sentiment of

"I can't do this. I don't know what to do. I give up."

Let's take it further. Imagine someone standing over a desk, arms spread wide. Aren't you immediately reminded of an animal claiming territory? Wide, expansive gestures signal confidence, assertiveness, and even dominance. If a person is standing with arms akimbo, they leave their torso exposed. This is a powerful way to communicate that they are confident in taking up room and don't feel threatened or unsure in the least.

Other gestures of confidence and assertiveness include that favorite of politicians and businessmen the world over: "hand steepling." The fingertips are pressed together so they form a little steeple. It's the classic negotiating gesture, signaling confidence, poise, and certainty about your power and position, as though the hands were merely resting and calmly contemplating their next move.

On the other hand (pun intended) wringing and rubbing the hands is more likely to demonstrate a lack of feeling in control or doubt in one's own abilities. Again, this is a pacifying gesture designed to release tension. Hands are our tools to effect change in the world and bring about our actions. When we fidget, wring our hands, or clench our fists, we are demonstrating a lack of ease and confidence in our abilities or find it difficult to act confidently.

What about the legs? These are often overlooked since they might be concealed under a desk, but legs and feet are powerful indicators too. "Happy feet" can bounce and jiggle—on the other hand, bouncy legs paired with other nervous or pacifying gestures may indicate an excess of nervous tension and energy or impatience . . . or too much coffee, you decide. Toes that point upward can be thought of as "smiling" feet and indicate positive, optimistic feelings.

Physiologically, our legs and feet are all about, unsurprisingly, movement. Busy feet could suggest an unexpressed desired to get moving, either literally or figuratively! It's also been said that feet point in the direction they unconsciously wish to go. Both toes turned toward the conversation partner can signal "I'm here with you; I'm present in this conversation" whereas feet angled toward an exit could be a clue that the person really would prefer to leave.

Other clues that someone is wanting to move, leave, or escape are gestures like clasping the knees, rocking up and down on the balls of the feet, or standing with a bit of a bounce in the step—all of these subtly communicate someone whose unconscious mind has "fired up the engines" and wants to get going. This could mean they're excited about possibilities and want to get started as soon as possible, or they may have a strong dislike for the current situation and almost literally want to "run away." Again, context matters!

Legs and feet can also reveal negative emotions. Crossing the legs, as with the arms, can signal a desire to close off or protect the body from a perceived threat or discomfort. Crossed legs are often tilted toward a person we like and trust—and away from someone we don't. This is because the legs can be used as a barrier, either warding off or welcoming in someone's presence. Women may dangle shoes off the tips of the toes in flirtatious moments, slipping a shoe on and off the heel again. Without getting too Freudian about it, the display of feet and legs can indicate comfort and even intimacy with someone. On the other hand, locking the feet and ankles can be part of a freeze response when someone *really* doesn't like a situation or person.

So having discussed the face, hands, legs and feet, and torso in general, what else is there? Turns out, a lot more. The body as a whole can be positioned in space in certain ways, held in certain postures, or brought further or closer to other people. The next time you meet someone new, lean in to shake their hand and then watch what they do with their entire body.

If they "stand their ground" and stay where they are, they're demonstrating comfort with the situation, you, and themselves. Taking a step back or turning the entire torso and feet to the side suggests that you may have gotten too close for their comfort. They may even take a step closer, signaling that they are happy with the contact and may even escalate it further.

The general principle is pretty obvious: bodies expand when they are comfortable, happy, or dominant. They contract when unhappy, fearful, or threatened. Bodies move toward what they like and away from what they don't like. Leaning toward a person can show agreement, comfort, flirtation, ease, and interest. Likewise, crossing the arms, turning away, leaning back, and using tightly crossed legs as a barrier show a person's unconscious attempt to get away from or protect themselves from something unwanted.

Those people who spread out on public transport? They feel relaxed, secure, and confident (annoying, isn't it?). Those that seem to bundle themselves as tightly as possible may instead signal low confidence and assertiveness, as though they were always trying to take up less room. Similarly puffing up the chest and holding out the arms in an aggressive posture communicates, "Look how big I am!" in an argument, whereas raising the shoulders and "turtling" in on oneself is nonverbally saying, "Please don't hurt me! Look how small I am!"

We're not much like gorillas in the forest, beating our chests during heated arguments—but if you look closely, you may still see faint clues to this more primal behavior anyway. Those postures that take up room and expand are all associated with dominance, assertiveness, and authority. Hands on the hips, hands held regally behind the back (doesn't it make you think of royalty or a dignified soldier who is unafraid of attack?), or even arms laced behind the neck as one leans back in a chair—all signify comfort and dominance.

When you are becoming aware of people's body language, ask in the first instance whether their actions, gestures, and postures are constricting or expanding. Is the face open or closed? Are the hands and arms spread wide and held loose and far from the body, or are the limbs kept close and tense? Is the facial expression you're looking at pulled tight or loose and open? Is the chin held high (sign of confidence) or tucked in (sign of uncertainty)?

Imagine you have no words at all to describe what you're looking at; just observe. Is the body in front of you relaxed and comfortable in space, or is there some tightness, tension, and unease in the way the limbs are held?

A lot of the art of body language is, once pointed out, rather intuitive. This is because each of us is actually already fluent in its interpretation. It is merely allowing ourselves to de-emphasize the verbal for a moment to take notice of the wealth of nonverbal information that's always flowing between people. None of it is really concealed. Rather, it's a question of opening up to data coming in on a channel we are not taught to pay attention to.

Putting it All Together

How can we use all of this to actually help us "read" people effectively and understand even those motivations, intentions, and feelings people may be actively trying to conceal? It's worth remembering right off the bat that detecting deception is not as straightforward as some would have you believe and, as we've seen, not as simple as spotting a tell-tale sign that proves a lie once and for all. Laypeople and professionals alike are notoriously bad at reading body language, despite the wealth of information we now have on the topic.

But the knack really comes in deciding what to do with certain observations once you've made them. Does a person's folded arms mean they're lying, unhappy about something, fearful . . . or just feeling cold? The trick comes in using not just one or two but a whole host of clues and tells to form a more comprehensive picture of behavior. The reason why it's so difficult to "spot a lie" with perfect accuracy is that the gestures and expressions associated with deception are often not different from those signifying stress or discomfort.

So given all this, is it worth learning to read body language? Absolutely. Adding this extra dimension to your interactions with others will only enrich your relationships and give you extra insight into your interpersonal conflicts and tensions. Knowing what's going on with another person allows you to be a better communicator and speak to what people are actually feeling rather than what they're merely saying.

Body language signals are always there. Every person is communicating nonverbally, at every moment of the day. And it is possible to not only observe this information in real-time but learn to properly synthesize and interpret it. You don't need to be an expert, and you don't need to be perfect. You just need to pay attention and be curious about your fellow human beings in a way you might not have before. As you're developing your body language reading skills, it may help to keep a few key principles in mind:

Establish normal behavior.

One or two gestures in a conversation don't mean much. They could be accidental or purely physiological. But the more you know how someone "normally" behaves, the more you can assume that any behavior outside of this is worth looking more closely at. If someone *always* squints their eyes, pouts, jiggles their feet, or clears their throat, you can more or less discount these gestures.

Look for unusual or incongruent behavior.

Reading people is about reading patterns of behavior. Pay special attention to clues that are unusual for that person. Suddenly fiddling with the hair and avoiding eye contact could tell you something is going on, especially if this person never does either of these things normally. You may with time come to recognize "tells" in people closest to you—they may always wrinkle their nose when being dishonest or clear their throat excessively when they're afraid and pretending not to be.

Importantly, pay close attention to those gestures and movements that seem incongruous. Discrepancies between verbal and nonverbal communication can tell you more than merely observing nonverbal communication alone. It's about context. An obvious example is someone wringing their hands, rubbing their temples, and sighing loudly but who claims, "I'm fine. Nothing's wrong." It's not the gestures that tell you this person is concealing distress, but the fact that they're incongruent with the words spoken.

Gather plenty of data.

As we've seen, certain constricting behaviors could merely be because one is cold, tired, or even ill, and expansive gestures may not be about confidence so much as feeling physically warm and wanting to cool off. This is why it's important to never interpret a gesture alone. Always consider clusters of clues.

If you see something, note it but don't come to any conclusions immediately. Look to see if they do it again. Look for other gestures that may reinforce what you've seen or else give evidence for the opposite interpretation. Check to see if the behavior repeats itself with other people or in other contexts. Take your time to really *analyze* the whole of what's in front of you.

Look for mirroring.

An important thing to remember is that certain gestures may mean one thing in one context or when shown to one person but have a different meaning in another context or with someone else. In other words, certain gestures could literally only apply to you as you speak to this person. If you're not very familiar with someone, a quick body language–reading shortcut is to merely notice whether they are or are not mirroring your gestures, whatever they are.

Mirroring is a fundamental human instinct; we tend to match and mimic the behavior and expressions of those we like or agree with, while we don't if we dislike a person or perceive them negatively. If you're in a meeting with a new client, you may notice that no matter how friendly your voice or how often you smile and make open-handed, warm gestures, they respond with coldness and closed gestures, failing to mirror back to you your optimism. Here, the gestures themselves are irrelevant; it's the fact that they are not shared which shows you that the person you're dealing with is unreceptive, hostile, or threatened.

Pay attention to energy.

This is not some fluffy, esoteric idea: in a group, simply take note of where intention, effort, and focus are being concentrated. Watch where energy flows. Sometimes, the "leader" of a group is only so in name; the real power may lie elsewhere. One only needs to look at how much focus and attention flows toward a baby in the room to see this in action—the baby says and does very little yet nevertheless commands the attention of everyone there. Similarly, a family may have the father as the official "leader," and he may gesture and talk loudly to cement this perception. But pay attention and you may see that it's his wife who is constantly deferred to, and every member of the family may show with their body language that it is in fact their mother's needs that take precedence, despite what's claimed verbally.

The most powerful voice in a room is not necessarily the loudest. A lot can be understood about the power dynamics in a group by watching to see where energy flows. Who speaks the most? Who are people always speaking *to*, and how? Who always seems to take "center stage"?

Remember that body language is dynamic.

When we speak, the content of our language isn't just about the words and the grammar we use to string them together. It's about *how* we talk. Do we say a lot or a little? What tone of voice? Are sentences long and complicated or short and terse? Is everything phrased tentatively, like a question, or is it stated confidently, as though it's a known fact? What's the speed of delivery? How loud? Is it clear or mumbling?

In the same way that verbal information can vary in the way it's communicated, nonverbal information can vary too. Gestures are not static, fixed things but living expressions that move in time and space. Watch the flow of information in real-time. Watch how expressions change and move in response to the environment and those in it. Don't be curious about "catching" a discreet gesture, but rather watch the flow of gestures as they change.

For example, look at how a person walks. Walking is like a body posture but set in motion. Shuffling, slow gaits suggest lack of confidence, while springy, quick ones suggest optimism and excitement. Become interested in how a person responds to others in conversation or their style of talking to those in positions of power. Once you start looking, you'll be amazed at the wealth of information that's just waiting there to be noticed.

Context is everything.

Finally, it bears repeating: no gesture occurs in a vacuum. Nonverbal communication needs to be considered in relation to everything else—just like verbal communication. Establish patterns and learn about a person's behavior over time, in different contexts, and toward different people. Consider the situation and environment—sweating and stuttering during your wedding vows or a big interview is understandable; doing so when asked to explain what you're doing snooping through someone's drawers is a little more suspicious.

Remember that everyone has their own unique, idiosyncratic personality. Factor into your analysis the fact that people are either introverted or extroverted, may favor emotions or intellect, may have high or low tolerance for risk and adversity, may thrive in stressful situations or wither in them, and may be spontaneous and casual or goal-directed and rather serious. Our instinctual, evolutionarily programmed impulses can't be hidden or resisted, but they can take on slightly different forms depending on our unique personalities.

Admittedly, reading facial expressions and body language is a skill that takes time and patience to master. There are no quick and easy tricks to understanding people's deeper motivations. However, remember the above principles and focus on honing your powers of observation, and you'll soon develop a knack for seeing and understanding even tiny ripples and flutters of behavior you might have previously missed. We live in a world dominated by words and language. But when you become a student of nonverbal communication, it's no exaggeration to say that you open yourself up to an entirely different, sometimes quite strange world.

The Human Body is a Whole—Read It that Way

Everyone has heard an offhand statistic which sounds a little something like, "Ninety percent of your communication is really nonverbal." We imagine that communication is primarily a question of language, symbols, noises and sounds, and images on a page, whereas the person creating the language is a separate physical entity occupying space.

But in reality, the boundary between verbal and non-verbal, medium and message, is always a little blurred.

In the previous sections, we've explicitly considered how a person can be "read" even beyond the content they are choosing to deliberately convey to you. In other words, you're not just listening to the message they're sending, but listening to *them*, as though their body itself were something to read and interpret.

In the discussion on detecting deceit or hidden true feelings, we made an assumption: that what is inside a person will invariably manifest itself somehow on the outside of a person. This is because we instinctively understand that human beings are *wholes*, i.e., the verbal and nonverbal are really just different aspects of the same thing. What really is the distinction between the words and the lips that say them? The body and the gesture that the body makes?

This may seem a little abstract, but it turns out there's now interesting research to back up the idea that communication as a whole can be understood as a complete expression of a human being. First of all, have you ever had a phone call with someone where you could instantly tell whether they were smiling or not? Call center managers will tell their staff that people can "hear smiles" over the phone, but how do you suppose this is actually possible?

It makes sense when we consider that a voice is not an abstract symbol, but a real, physiological part of the human body.

Researcher at the Donders Institute of Radboud University Wim Pouw published some interesting findings in the *PNAS* journal in 2020. He was interested in the topic we all seem to instinctively understand: that hand gestures and facial expressions can help us better understand what is being communicated—in fact at times a gesture can be fundamental to us understanding the message.

In an experiment, Pouw asked six people to make a simple noise (like "aaaaa") but to pair it with different arm and hand gestures as they spoke. He then asked thirty other participants to listen to recordings of the sounds only. Surprisingly, the participants were able to guess what the accompanying movements were and even mimic them for themselves. They could say what the movement was, where it was performed and even how quickly the gesture was made!

How? Pouw's theory is that people are able to unconsciously detect subtle but important shifts in voice pitch and volume, as well as speed changes, that accompany different gestures. When you make a gesture, your *whole body* gets involved, including your voice. In other words, when you hear a voice, you are hearing multiple aspects about that person's body.

When speaking, sound vibrates all through the connective tissues of your body, but differences in muscle tension can arise if we are making gestures with other parts of our body, and we can hear these tiny adjustments in the voice. The great thing about this particular skill is that you don't necessarily need to train it, just become aware of it. You probably never thought you could practice reading body language over the phone, but you can—if you understand that the voice is simply a part of a person's body!

Voice alone is an incredibly rich aspect of behavior to study. When you hear someone from another room, on a recording or over the phone, close your eyes and imagine what their body is doing, and what that posture or gesture might indicate. You can undoubtedly hear age and sex through voice, too, but you can also infer something about a person's ethnicity or nationality by listening to their accent or vocabulary.

Listen to the speed, timbre, volume, pitch and degree of control used. How is the person breathing? How are their words and the *way* they're saying those words reinforcing one another, or perhaps undermining one another? For example someone on the phone might be telling you how excited they are about something, but their slow and sluggish voice may suggest to you that they're slouching and folded in on themselves—and greatly overstating their excitement.

Thinking in Terms of Message Clusters

Let's shift our attention away from individual physical actions that may or not mean or suggest something else, and instead consider human behavior in terms of the overall message it communicates to others. If we are feeling hostile and aggressive, for example, this attitude and intention will show up in every area, from our language to our actions to our facial expressions to our voice. Rather than trying to imagine what every possible manifestation of aggression looks like, we can focus on the aggression itself, and watch for resulting clusters of behavior.

Aggression is understandably shown by confronting gestures, or those that move actively and energetically *towards* a target. Invasive, approaching gestures that move in on another person can signify an attempt to dominate, control or attack. Verbally, this could look like an insult or a jeer, physically it looks like standing too close, or even displaying or exposing oneself as if to demonstrate superior strength. Aggression is all about sudden, impactful and targeted gestures. It's as though the entire body is clenched around a single pointed intention.

Assertive body language, on the other hand, is as forceful but not so directed. This is a person standing their ground, i.e., being firm, balanced, smooth and open in expression of a confidently held desire. The aggressive person may yell, whereas an assertive one may simply state their business with a kind of muscular certainty that can be heard in the voice.

Submissive body language is the complement—look for "lowering," self-protective gestures that make the person seems smaller, with small, appeasing gestures like smiling excessively, being motionless, speaking quietly, turning the eyes downward or assuming a vulnerable or non-threatening stance.

This is different from being genuinely **open and receptive**. Relaxed, friendly people will signal looseness—open and uncrossed arms and legs, unguarded facial expressions, easy speech, or even loosening or removing outer layers of clothing to show informality.

This is a little like **romantic** body language, except someone who is sexually interested will also behave in ways that emphasize intimacy. The focus will be on sensuality (touching the other person or the self, preening, stroking, slowing down, warm smiles) and connection (prolonged eye contact, questions, agreement, mirroring). The overwhelming perception is that of an invitation to close distance.

Deceptive body language is anything that is characterized by a sense of tension. Deceit is the existence of two conflicting things—for example someone believes one thing but says another. Look for the tension that such a disparity creates. You want to look for anxiety, closed body language, and a sense of distractedness (after all, they are processing extra data they don't want to reveal to you!). Look for someone who appears to be trying hard to control themselves, with an anxious effect.

By looking at intentions behind overall communication, we can start to read the body as a whole. This makes it easier to gather multiple data points more quickly, and find patterns of behavior rather than inferring too much from just a single gesture or expression. Consider the entire human body—the limbs, the face, the voice, the posture, the torso, the clothing, the hair, the hands and fingers, everything.

Can you see a cluster of closed off, defensive gestures? Is someone trying to display power, strength and dominance? Or are they just confident? Is the person in front of you trying to show that they are trustworthy, or that they have a truly valuable thing to sell you (salesman's body language) or that they are greeting you with openness and respect?

In very general terms, look for the following *whole body* patterns:

- Crossing, closing in, or shutting off – could signal guardedness, suspicion, shyness
- Expanding, opening, loosening – signals friendliness, comfort, trust, relaxation
- Forward, pointed, directed – may speak to dominance, control, persuasiveness
- Preening, touching, stroking – shows romantic intentions
- Striking, abruptness, force, loudness – signal energy or violence, sometimes fear
- Repeating, agreement, mirroring – shows respect, friendliness, admiration, submission

In an even broader sense, look at overall behavior and communication as an expression of holding—holding on to, holding in, holding up, holding back, failing to hold, holding tightly, etc. If you meet someone whose entire being seems to be an expression of force and control (holding onto), you can take your interpretation of them from here, and better understand all the smaller data points—the hand wringing, the tightened and pursed lips, the furrowed brow, the shallow breathing that seems to strangle the voice, the high pitched tone, the rapid blinking . . .

Their body is sending you one clear, uniform message: one of tension. There's something big going on that they're trying hard to keep under wraps. Further context clues could tell you whether this is an uncomfortable admission, a lie, or simply something they're embarrassed about sharing with you.

Takeaways

- Finally, we get right into the thick of it. How can we read and analyze people just through sight and observation? We cover two primary aspects: facial expressions and body language. It's important to note that though many aspects have been scientifically proven (with physiological origins), we can't say that simple observations are foolproof. It can never be definitive because there are too many external factors to take into account. But we can better understand what typical things to look for and what we can glean from them.

- We use two types of facial expressions: micro- and macroexpressions. Macroexpressions are larger, slower, and more obvious. They are also routinely faked and consciously created. Microexpressions are the opposite of all of those things: incredibly quick, almost unperceivable, and unconscious. Psychologist Paul Ekman identified a host of microexpressions for each of the six basic emotions and in particular has also identified microexpressions to indicate nervousness, lying, or deception.

- Body language has a much broader range of possible interpretations.

Generally, a relaxed body takes up space, while an anxious body contracts and wants to conceal and comfort itself. There are too many specifics to list in a bullet point, but just keep in mind that the only true way to analyze body language is to first know exactly what someone is like when they are normal.

- To put everything together, we need to read the body as a whole, and look for general clusters of behavior that work together to communicate a unified message. The voice can be thought of as a part of the body, and read like other body language. Look for signs or cues that are incongruent and don't mesh well with the other cues they're giving, this might reveal that the other person is trying to hide something if you can notice other cues that reaffirm this conclusion. However, as always, the signs you've picked up on could well be meaningless, so make sure you have enough data to support them.

Chapter 3. Personality Science and Typology

Just as we can understand any kind of communication, behavior or speech from a person as a direct expression of their *total* selves, we can include personality into the mix, too. Personality can be thought of as a persistent pattern of behavior over the long term. You might read a certain gesture or tone of voice to mean XYZ, but that same gesture or voice, when repeated reliably and often enough, starts to cement into a persona.

It follows then that if we know a little about the persistent, lifelong pattern of *general* behavior, we have more context to help us understand the *specific* behavior we see in front of us at any one time. In psychological terms, personality is usually understood as a special blend of a person's unique traits, i.e., where they fall on multiple attitudinal continuums.

Most personality theories are interested in the fundamental axes on which people differ—if you can get a handle on these basic nuts and bolts of human personality, the idea is that you gain greater insight into the behavior, perhaps even learning to pre-empt and predict it.

Test Your Personality

Now, any discussion of analyzing personality and identity would be incomplete without delving into the Big Five personality traits, as well as the Meyers-Briggs Type Indicator and associated Keirsey Temperaments. These are direct ways of understanding who someone is, to the extent that such tests can be accurate.

Very rarely will you possess this amount of knowledge about someone you want to read or analyze, but again, it's worth understanding a few different scales upon which to evaluate others. You might be able to identify some of these traits in others and then understand their motivations and values as a result.

Chances are, at some point in your life, you've taken a personality, career aptitude, or relationship test to learn more about yourself. In the context of analyzing people, this isn't quite going to get us where we want. Using these personality tests almost defeats the purpose of analyzing someone based on observations and behaviors, but they do provide plenty of food for thought in exactly what traits to look for and what differentiates people.

Hopefully, you've stumbled across one that sought to evaluate you based on the Big Five personality traits. As previously mentioned, this is a theory that breaks down the human psyche into five broad characteristics. These five simple factors could determine the very complex question

you've been chasing: what makes you *you*—
and what makes other people *them*?

The Big Five

It's a theory that dates back to 1949, in research published by D.W. Fiske. Since then, it's been gaining popularity and has been written about by the likes of Norman (1967), Smith (1967), Goldberg (1981), and McCrae and Costa (1987). Instead of evaluating you as a whole based on your experiences and motivations, this theory reduces you down to five traits: openness to experience, conscientiousness, extroversion, agreeableness, and neuroticism.

You may have heard of these before. Terms like introvert and extrovert are thrown around a lot these days, but what do they really mean? They're two ends of the spectrum. Each trait has two extremes, and although we may not want to admit it, every one of us embodies all of these five traits to some degree. According to this theory, it's how much of each and where we land in the range between the extremes that determine our unique personality.

Openness to Experience. The first of the Big Five personality traits determines how willing you are to take risks or try something new. Would you ever jump out of a plane? How about pack up and move halfway around the world to immerse yourself in a new culture? If your answer to both of those questions was a resounding yes, then you probably score high in your openness to experience. You seek out the unknown.

At one extreme, people who are high in openness are curious and imaginative. They go in search of new adventures and experiences. They can get bored easily and turn to their creativity to uncover new interests and even daring activities. These people are flexible and seek out variety in their daily life. For them, routine is not an option. At the other end of the spectrum, people who are low on the openness scale prefer continuity and stability to change. They are practical, sensible, and more conventional than their peers. Change is not their friend.

In the real world, most people fall somewhere between these opposites, but where you find yourself on the spectrum could reveal a lot about who you are and what you excel at.

Do you dream of being a CEO or at the head of your field, for instance? Openness has been linked to leadership. If you're able to entertain new ideas, think outside the box, and adapt quickly to new situations, you're more likely to become and succeed as a leader (Lebowitz, 2016).

It was Apple cofounder Steve Jobs's decision to audit a calligraphy class in 1973 that would lead to the groundbreaking typography in Mac computers years later. At the time, no one associated computers with beautiful fonts, but Jobs saw something that no one else could. He embraced the calligraphy class, sought to change the way people thought about computers, and opened himself up to a new vision of the future.

Conscientiousness. This is the personality trait that makes you careful and cautious. You're vigilant in your actions and often think twice, or three times, before making a decision, especially if it wasn't in your original plans.

People who have high levels of conscientiousness tend to be extremely focused on their goals. They plan things out, focusing on the detailed tasks at hand, and they stick to their schedules. They have better control over their impulses, emotions, and behaviors, such that they are able to focus more of their energy on their professional success. While they may not live as adventurously as their peers, they do tend to live longer, thanks in part to their healthier habits.

At the other end of the spectrum, people who are not so conscientious tend to be more impulsive and disorganized. They become demotivated by too much structure, can procrastinate on important work, and have a weaker ability to control their behavior. This can lead to more self-destructive habits, such as smoking and substance abuse, and an overall inability to get things done. Impulse control is no easy feat for them.

So how conscientious are you? Do you like schedules at work but still find yourself avoiding exercise when you get home? You may embrace some aspects of conscientiousness, like schedules and to-do lists, and not others, like exercising or performing other healthy habits. Most people land somewhere in the middle of the conscientiousness spectrum, but if you can find ways to embrace planning and order a little bit more, you could be setting yourself up for success.

Conscientiousness has been linked to better success after training (Woods, Patterson, Koczwara & Sofat, 2016), more effective job performance (Barrick & Mount, 1991), higher job satisfaction, and careers with greater prestige and higher incomes (Judge, Higgins, Thoresen & Barrick, 1999). A study by Soldz and Vaillant (1999) also found that high levels of conscientiousness have helped people better adjust to the challenges of life that will inevitably sneak up on you.

Conscientiousness is the preventative medicine we could all use to stop problems before they start.

Extroversion. This is the trait that defines how outgoing or social you are. Extroverts are easy to spot. They're the life of the party, they've got lots of energy, and they know how to talk. Extroverts draw their energy from being around other people and thrive on being the center of attention. For that reason, they maintain a wide circle of friends and take every opportunity to meet new people.

At the other extreme are people who often find extroverts exhausting to be around: introverts. Why spend time trying to make conversation with large groups of people when you can be at home with your own thoughts? Introverts aren't shy; they simply prefer solitude to socializing or calm to chaos.

Do you wish office parties would never end, or do you feel drained after about an hour?

Do you enjoy meeting new people, or would you prefer to be cuddled up at home with a good book? Are you a morning person, or do you truly wake up when the sun goes down?

If you're often the last one to leave a social gathering, you enjoy being around people, and you thrive on the late-night hours, you likely rank high on the extroversion scale. If, on the other hand, you dread the thought of going to parties, would rather stay home alone, and prefer to wake up bright and early to start your day, you're probably more of an introvert.

Depending on the day, you may be inclined to go either way. However, by and large, people typically place somewhere along the spectrum between the two.

Agreeableness. This is the trait that identifies how kind and sympathetic you are and how warm and cooperative you are with others.

Do you tend to take a big interest in other people and their problems? When you see others going through difficulties, does it affect you, too? If you're empathetic and caring toward others and driven by the desire to help, you may be quite an agreeable person. You feel their pain and are driven to do something about it.

At the other end of the spectrum, people who are less agreeable may find they take less of an interest in other people's lives. Instead of trying to work together to solve a problem, they may be more content to go it alone. They're not agreeable because they are determined to do exactly what they want to do. Because of their nature, they may often be perceived as offensive or unpleasant to be around.

We all have different thresholds for how much we're willing to do for others and how much we're willing to work together. That limit is where you rank on the agreeableness spectrum.

Why people are so agreeable is still up for debate. For some, it's the genuine concern for the well-being of others. For others, it's the result of social pressure and accepted norms. Fear of consequences can be a motivating factor. Some agreeable people may be acting that way because they are petrified of social confrontation. Whatever the case, research has shown that agreeable people are rarely cruel, ruthless, or selfish (Roccas, Sagiv, Schwartz & Knafo, 2002). If you're looking for ways to be a little bit happier, figuring out where you lie on the agreeable index may be a good way to start.

Neuroticism. We all have those days when nothing is how it seems. You think your coworkers are out to get you. You're so anxious you can't sleep. You feel like you're caught in a Woody Allen film. But if you find yourself having lots of those days, to the point where you feel more down than you do up, you may have high levels of the last of the Big Five traits: neuroticism. This is the personality trait that essentially measures how emotionally stable you are. It identifies your ability to remain steady and balanced versus anxious, insecure, or constantly distracted.

Neurotics tend to approach life with a high dose of anxiety. They worry more than most and their moods can shift quickly and with little prompting. This kind of behavior can make them prone to being stressed or even depressed.

Those on the less neurotic side of the spectrum tend to be more emotionally stable. When stress comes their way, they have an easier time dealing with it. Bouts of sadness are few and far between, and they see fewer reasons to stress about whatever may come their way.

Do you find yourself using humor to cope with a challenge, or do problems tend to stress you out? Are you pretty levelheaded all day long, or do you switch from hot to cold in a heartbeat? If you take things in stride and usually only have one mood per day, you're probably less neurotic than others. But if you have many moods in the space of a short amount of time and are anxious more often than not, you're probably on the more neurotic side.

However, being neurotic doesn't have to be all doom and gloom. After all, worrying about our health is what keeps us taking vitamins and visiting the doctor's office for checkups. In that case, the anxiety of neurotics may actually keep them one step ahead in many ways.

In the end, we have five scales that have been proven to at least be major elements of personality for you to evaluate people on. Let's say you start working with a new business partner, and are warned by others ahead of time that this person can be really rude and difficult to work with. In conversation, you do notice they're a little cold and blunt. They don't seem to observe social niceties. After a month of working with them, you understand that this is more a question of their personality—it's a pattern of behavior that shows itself to all people, in all contexts.

You remember this when in your next meeting and you suggest a somewhat controversial idea. Your business partner immediately seems a little hostile and unconvinced. They cross their arms, frown a little.

Another person might have assumed this body language was a direct rejection of their idea, but you, understanding this person's *personality as a baseline*, can read

146

it for what it is: business as usual. You continue to assert your suggestion and are not surprised when your partner eventually agrees with enthusiasm, despite initially appearing quite stern and uncommunicative.

In this way, personality is yet another (powerful) data point to help you interpret and make sense of the information you're confronted with in the moment. Another such personality tool is the Myers-Briggs Type Indicator (MBTI) as well as the subsequent Keirsey Temperaments.

Jung and the MBTI

The MBTI has been one of the most popular methods for people to evaluate and categorize themselves—of course, this means we should understand it to categorize *others*. Overall, the test is based on four very distinct *dichotomies*, which you can imagine as simply being traits, similar to the Big Five traits. People have compared the MBTI as one that purely functions as a modern horoscope. Of course, no test is foolproof, and this doesn't mean that it still can't provide you important insight into a person's character or identity.

The MBTI was developed around the time of World War II. Myers and Briggs were two housewives and observed many people taking job opportunities willy-nilly. However, it bothered them that many of those people were taking jobs that didn't necessarily pertain to their skills. They combined their observations with the work of psychologist Carl Jung, who believed that archetypes came from models of people, behavior, and their personalities. He strongly suggested that these archetypes came innately due to the influence of human behavior.

Thus, the MBTI was developed with the intention of helping people find jobs and careers that were better suited to their innate personalities. As mentioned, there are four general dichotomies or traits:

- For personality, the spectrum is extroverted (E) to introverted (I).

- For perception, the spectrum is sensing (S) to intuition (N).
- For judging, the spectrum is thinking (T) to feeling (F).
- For implementation, the spectrum is judging (J) to perceiving (P).

The idea is that everyone can measure themselves along these four spectrums, and certain patterns will emerge so that you are able to discover your personality type.

The first dichotomy, extroversion versus introversion, signifies the source as well as the direction of a person's energy expression. Note that this is defined slightly differently from the Big Five trait of extroversion.

An extrovert and his energy expression mainly happen in the external world. When in the presence and company of others, extroverts are able to recharge. For an introvert, his source of energy mainly happens in his internal world. Having space to himself or herself is ideal and can prove to be the best mode of recharging that energy expression.

Extroverted people are action-oriented in comparison to introverted people, who are more thought-oriented. For instance, in a classroom, extroverted students like to participate in group discussions and presentations. Their interactions with other students provide that sense of charge for their personality types. An introverted student would rather work alone on projects and feel somewhat uncomfortable during whole class discussions. They like being able to think on their own and work through assessments by themselves as well.

The second dichotomy, sensing versus intuition, represents how someone perceives information.

When a person is sensing, he or she believes information received directly from that external world. This may come in the form of using his or her five senses—sight, smell, touch, taste, and hearing. Decisions come in more immediate and experienced-based ways.

For someone using intuition, he or she believes information from an internal world—their intuition—over external evidence. This comes in the form of having that "gut feeling." He or she digs a little deeper into detail and tries to connect patterns. It may take a little longer before a decision can be made.

Sensing has to do with believing information that is more concrete and tangible over intuition, which is more about looking at the underlying theories or principles that may come out of data. A police officer will always use evidence and data to support their claims for making an arrest because this information is measurable. On the other side, a lawyer would exhibit more intuition because there could be a lot more to the context being presented, which helps him defend his clients.

The third dichotomy, thinking versus feeling, has to do with how a person processes information. Thinking is when someone makes a decision mainly through the process of logical thinking. They also think in tangible means, where they look to rules to guide their decision-making.

Opposite to this is the feeling where someone would rather make a decision based on emotion. For decisions, these people look to what they value as a means for choosing their best option. They may deem thinkers as being cold and heartless.

Thinking mostly occurs when someone lays out all the possible and practical reasons for making a sound decision. Basically, someone is going to make a decision using one's brain. Feeling is when someone will make that decision from the heart. People who purchase homes will either sign the paperwork based on pricing and resale value (thinking) versus those buying to stay in their old neighborhoods (feeling).

The fourth dichotomy, judging versus perceiving, is how someone will implement the information he has processed.

Organizing life events is how someone would judge and later use it, as a rule, to stick to the plan. These people like to have order and structure. Their sense of self-control comes from being able to control their environments as much as possible. Judging types will normally use previous experiences as a catalyst to either continue or avoid certain behaviors later. They also like to see things settled and done with.

Improvisation and option exploration is what someone would do with perceiving. These people like having options and see organization as being a limit to their potential. They like to make choices when they are necessary and like to explore problem-solving and strategizing. Perceiving types will somewhat live in the moment and understand that there are multitudes of options available to them, regardless of how other experiences have occurred in the past.

There are a total of sixteen different combinations, or personality types, that can come out of the permutations of preferences in the mentioned four dichotomies. These help to represent one of the two poles that each person can have in terms of a dominant dichotomy. So this is what defines the sixteen different personality types, as each can be assigned a four-letter acronym.

So for instance, ESFJ would stand for extroverted, sensing, feeling, and judging. These people might be those you see on television sitcoms who gossip about everyone and whose main goal in life is to be married with kids, only to be able to gossip with other moms around the neighborhood. Of course, this is a categorization so stereotypical that it hurts, but nonetheless, observing and categorizing someone based on these four simple letters can unlock a deeper understanding of anyone.

A vast shortcoming is that the MBTI only gives answers that are definitive, and it doesn't account for the fact that people are usually not one-sided on their traits. People aren't entirely on one end of the spectrum over another. The MBTI only gives people two ends of the spectrum, not anything in between. Thus, most people can be moderate in many other traits. For instance, you might be forty-five percent extroverted and fifty-five percent introverted, but the MBTI would call you an introvert without subtlety.

Another shortcoming rests not with the MBTI itself, but with the fact that we are all changing throughout our lifetimes. Professor David Pittenger of Marshall University found that when a retest of the MBTI is conducted over a short amount of time, as many as fifty percent of people will get classified into a different type. Over time and as expected, people can change. Results from their MBTIs can change in a span of either days or weeks depending on their moods or influences from their external and internal environments. These factors will say nothing about their actual personality types.

How can we use this theory practically, in our day to day encounters with people? Sadly, it's not at all easy to simply guess what someone's MBTI type would be (though many people do with wild abandon!). Since we can't give everyone we meet a full written version of the test, we need to try and use the broad strokes of the theory to gain a general and more ad-hoc understanding of people in natural contexts.

Try it yourself: the next time you meet someone new, try to determine whether they're more introverted or extroverted (or in the middle somewhere?). Note their body language, their behavior, and all the context clues available to you. Next, ask yourself if they're likely more intuitive or sensing. The tactile, practical and direct person may be more sensing than the "big picture" thinker who is more prone to saying "well, that's complicated" to every question, no matter how simple.

To determine whether they're more thinking or feeling inclined, listen to their language, the content of their speech, and where their focus goes. Are they engaging you on facts, ideas, abstract plans? Or are they talking about people and relationships? To tell the judging from the perceiving types, take a note of the general attitude towards life—do they seem loose, open-ended, uncommitted? Or do you get the feeling this person is constantly making decisions, and always has a plan or is about to make one?

Honing in on people using just one or two of these aspects is enough to narrow down potential personalities. As always, watch out for your biases and assumptions (for example, the person is not in the least feeling oriented, it's just a relaxed environment and they have a massive crush on you!). You could test your theory in the moment by adjusting your communication style and observing the results.

You'll know you're talking to a more thinking person when they respond better to a fascinating new idea you share but find your endearing personal anecdote a bit boring, for example. If the person you're in conversation with keeps wanting to bring the discussion round to a definitive conclusion, you could guess they are closer to the J side than the P. Again, however, it's all about context.

It's also worth remembering that different environments tend to bring different personality traits to the surface. Your spouse is almost certainly going to be communicating more with a preference towards feelings when discussion your marriage than when at their workplace, and this has nothing to do with their feeling/thinking orientation.

Keirsey's Temperaments

One popular way of understanding the MBTI is through David Keirsey's four temperaments. He helped to organize the information people received from the MBTI to narrow it down from sixteen personality types to four general temperaments instead. Within each temperament Keirsey also identified two types of roles one might play instinctively and naturally.

Temperament One: The Guardian

This happens when someone results in being a sensor and judger. These people have a longing to belong, contribute to their society, and are confident in their own abilities.

Guardians are also concrete and more organized. They seek security and belonging while still being concerned with responsibilities and duties. Logistics is one of their greatest strengths; they are excellent at organization, facilitation, supporting, and checking. Their two roles are administrators and conservators.

Administrators tend to be the proactive and directive versions of guardians. They are most efficient in regulating. Conservators are the reactive and expressive versions of guardians and their best intelligence is supporting.

Temperament Two: The Artisan

This occurs when an individual tests as being a sensor and perceiver. These individuals live freely and through a lot of action-filled events.

Artisans are completely adaptable. They usually seek out stimulation and virtuosity. Artisans are highly concerned with making a large impact, and one of their greatest strengths happens to be tactics. They are extremely proficient in troubleshooting, problem-solving, and agility. They also have the ability to manipulate tools, instruments, and equipment.

Artisans have two roles—operators and entertainers. Operators are the directive and proactive version of artisans. They have a high capacity to expedite and are the attentive crafters and promoters of the role variants. Entertainers are the more informative and reactive versions of artisans. They have a great way of improvising and are attentive to details.

Keirsey estimates that about eighty percent of the population is categorized as being artisans or guardians.

Temperament Three: The Idealist

This happens when someone results in being an intuitive and feeler. These people find meaning in their lives while helping themselves and others be the best versions of themselves. They value uniqueness and individuality.

Idealists are abstract and can be compassionate. They work to seek significance and meaning in almost everything. They are concerned with their own personal growth and being able to find their true identities. They are very good at diplomacy and have strengths in clarifying, unifying, individualizing, and inspiring others. They have two roles—mentors and advocates.

Mentors are the proactive and directive versions of idealists. They are very good at developing and their attentive variant roles are counselors and teachers. Advocates are the reactive and informative idealists who are very good at mediating.

Temperament Four: The Rational

This occurs when someone tests as being an intuitive and thinker. There is always a drive to increase these people's knowledge and they are highly competent. They usually have a sense of personal satisfaction.

Rationals are objective and abstract. They seek to be masters of their craft and have self-control. They are usually concerned with their own type of knowledge and competence. Strategy is their greatest strength, and they have the ability to logically investigate, engineer, conceptualize, theorize, and coordinate. Their two roles are coordinators and engineers.

Coordinators are the proactive and directive versions of rationals. They are great at arranging and their variant roles are masterminds and field marshals. Engineers are the reactive and informative versions of rationals.

Keirsey's temperaments have the ability to take personality trait assessment a few steps deeper than that of the MBTI. It helps to evaluate a person's results as they relate to other traits while the MBTI focuses on each trait individually. But like the MBTI, no individual can ever be just one temperament. Almost every single person will have traits in all temperaments, so it would be extremely difficult to pinpoint just one category.

Temperaments overall have the ability to give people a better sense into how they are and what they can do to change their personalities. Being a personality type merely tells someone how they are, but temperaments look beyond that surface-level interpretation. Temperament identification allows people to score themselves and potentially make a change for the better. They have more self-awareness about themselves and can better adapt if needed.

Both tests have the ability to yield useful information and at least give you a place to start from in analyzing someone. Depending on some tentative initial observations, you could change the way you communicate with a person, the questions you ask, and the way you speak. This could help you surreptitiously gather more information, essentially using your engagement with someone as an ongoing experiment where you test and re-test your hypotheses about them.

This not so cold as it sounds; in fact, people who are naturally gifted at this kind of people-reading are often experienced by others as more interesting, likeable, attractive, intelligent and empathetic. For example, if you were talking to someone you suspected was an idealist, you might make sure to compliment them in ways you know they would appreciate: you'd tell them that they were kind or doing good work in the world.

If you were having a disagreement with someone who was sending strong clues that they might be an artisan, you might try to resolve the conflict by referring to the practical benefits of doing so, rather than appealing to "logic," trying to push their emotional buttons or making an appeal to convention or authority.

We turn to the last one of our personality tests in the Enneagram, which functions similarly to Keirsey's temperaments.

The Enneagram

The Enneagram test was developed in the 1960s as a way for people to attain *self-actualization*. The focus is primarily on self-improvement because it forces people to face their own faults head-on. What makes it unique is that it aims to identify the *how* and *why* rather than the *what* people do. Rather than dive into the minutiae, it's helpful to have a broad overview of the types of possible outcomes from the Enneagram and try to spot yourself in them.

There are nine types that can be identified when taking this test.

Type One—The Reformer. These types of people are usually concerned with always being right and have a high level of integrity. They can also be deemed as being judgmental and self-righteous. Examples include priests and doctors.

Type Two—The Helper. These people have a yearning to be loved and appreciated. They are usually very generous but can also be seen as manipulative and prideful. Examples include mothers and teachers.

Type Three—The Achiever. These types of people love to be praised and applauded. They are workaholics, which can make them narcissistic and vain. Examples include actors and students.

Type Four—The Individualist. Typically, these types will search for meaning in their lives with a need to be unique. They are certainly creative but can also be moody and temperamental. Examples include musicians and painters.

Type Five—The Investigator. These people strive to be knowledgeable and competent. Most of the time, they are very objective, but they have the tendency to hoard themselves away. An example includes researchers.

Type Six—The Loyalist. These people are thoughtful in their planning and are very loyal to anyone they care about. They do question everything, and this can make them suspicious and paranoid. Examples include survivalists and police officers.

Type Seven—The Enthusiast. These types of people like adventure and are very energetic. They make the best of everything, and this can force them to be reckless and overindulgent. Examples include thrill-seekers and actors.

Type Eight—The Challenger. These people always have to be in control or have power. They are assertive, which can come off as being aggressive and extreme. Examples include overbearing parents or people in the military.

Type Nine—The Peacemaker. Lastly, these people are stable and mediate situations. They're normally easygoing and accepting of all things. But this type of naive behavior can make them oblivious to negative things happening around them. Examples include hippies and grandparents.

Some people may exhibit a bit of each of these types or be more dominant in just a few. Taking the test allows people to gain a better understanding of themselves and why they act the way they do in certain situations. The test forces people to look at themselves in a deeper way that could potentially unlock unconscious ways of thinking.

Consider these personality tests the theoretical introduction to reading and analyzing people, because the process is as follows: understand various test scales, observe people, and then see where people might fit. In the end, you might gain useful information, but you also might be trying to shoehorn people into incorrect categories or are overall wrong about your perception.

To make sure you're using these theories to their best advantage, you need to remember that they are simply models, nothing more. Models have limitations, and they are always oversimplifications of complex phenomena. A personality theory or idea can help make it easier to explain or understand the complex creature called a human being, but you need to be ready to continue gathering data and adjusting your perceptions as you go.

Let's say the person you met yesterday really struck you as a type eight enneagram, the challenger. In your conversation at work with them yesterday, you noticed their forceful and directed body language—firm voice, imposing posture, interrupting you, direct eye contact, set jaw and piercing gaze. But then when you meet them today, out of work, you notice that their body language actually seems more anxious to you. Could their apparent forcefulness be a mask?

On further conversations, you switch models and start to understand that this person is not forceful at all, but simply confident and direct in their communication. You start to see them as a focused, enthusiastic "rational" type whose extroversion is high but conscientiousness and agreeableness relatively low. When you start to engage with them bearing all this in mind, you suddenly notice yourself really "clicking" and find you soon become pretty close friends!

Takeaways

- We start our journey into analyzing people like a psychologist by first taking a look at the various personality tests and seeing what we can glean from them. It turns out, quite a bit, although they can't be said to be definitive measures or categories of people. Mostly, they provide different scales and perspectives through which to view people differently.

- The Big Five personality traits are one of the first attempts to classify people based on specific traits rather than as a whole. You can remember the traits easily with the acronym OCEAN: openness to experience (trying new things), conscientiousness (being cautious and careful), extroversion (drawing energy from others and social situations), agreeableness (warm and sympathetic), and neuroticism (anxious and high-strung).

- Next, the MBTI, though helpful as a guideline, can sometimes suffer from people treating it like a horoscope and reading into their type what they wish to see about themselves. The MBTI functions on four distinct traits and how much of each trait you are or are not. The traits are generally introverted/extroverted (your general attitude toward others), intuitive/feeling (how you perceive information), thinking/feeling (how you process information), and perceiving/judging (how you implement information). Thus, this creates sixteen distinct personality types.

- The MBTI does suffer from some shortcomings, including the usage of stereotyping to classify people, and the lack of consistency when people score differently depending on their current moods and circumstances.

- The Keirsey temperaments are a way of organizing the same information gleaned from the MBTI. Here, there are four distinct temperaments, each with two types of roles instead of sixteen personality types. The four temperaments are guardian, artisan, idealistic, and rational. Keirsey estimated that up to eighty percent of the population fell into the first two temperaments.

- Finally, the Enneagram is the final personality test we cover in this chapter. It is composed of nine general types of personalities: reformer, helper, achiever, individualist, investigator, loyalist, enthusiast, challenger, and peacemaker. Each type is composed of a specific set of traits, and in this way, it functions more similarly to Keirsey's temperaments.

Chapter 4. Lie Detection 101 (and Caveats)

So far in this book, we've thought about all the different motivations that compel people to act and engage with others, all the ways their needs can influence their communication and actions, how the ego plays into the mix, and all the many ways we can "read between the lines" and consider the total body when listening to everything a person is "saying."

Doing so, we can peer more deeply into people, and understand them better. But let's be honest, a big part of this "understanding" is not just coming from innocent curiosity. Many of us have a (legitimate) need to understand people better so we can detect when they are manipulating us, hiding something, or outright lying.

Being a good judge of character and an excellent people-reader makes you a great friend, lover, parent or colleague. But it also protects you from the less-than-noble intentions of others. Whether it's uncovering white lies in your personal life, seeing through underhanded dating tactics, or getting to the bottom of someone who wants to actively misdirect you (big shoutout to the entire advertising industry), the skills we've considered so far can be a powerful self-defense strategy.

At this point in the book, you're probably sick of hearing the caveat, but it bears repeating: in people-reading, there are no guarantees. There are observations, theories, and best guesses, but no technique is one hundred percent guaranteed to work for everyone, since we all have different mannerisms, personalities, backgrounds, etc.

Rather, what we cover in this chapter is a great starting point; yet one more tool to put in the toolkit, one more lens through which to view the data. We'll take a look at how professional lie-detectors do the work, i.e., FBI and CIA agents, interrogators and police officers who need to be as accurate as possible in sometimes very short spaces of time.

The Problem: Uncertainty

Just like it seems that everyone believes they're an above average driver, most people seem to think they're good at spotting liars—when they may not be. A 2006 study in the *Forensic Examiner* journal found, in fact, that people were generally quite bad at detecting liars, and it didn't matter their age, their education levels, gender or confidence in being able to sniff out deceit. In fact, even professionally trained lie detectors were no better when it came down to it.

Another 2006 paper in the *Personality and Social Psychology Review* said most people, even psychologists and judges, were no better at deception detection than mere chance. Some estimates say just fifty in twenty thousand people are able to spot a liar more than eighty of the time—a pretty dismal success rate! Though nobody likes to think that they're especially easy to deceive, the fact is that a practiced liar can be extremely convincing. And this is where we start with our chapter on becoming a better human lie detector: with caution.

The trouble is that the things we typically rely on to help us read people—facial expressions, body language, word choice—can always show a degree of variability. The assumption is that lying people will all present themselves in the same predictable way, when it's clear that individual differences are so broad as to make these observational tips and tricks close to useless. While the techniques we've discussed in previous chapters can tell us plenty about the personality of a sincere person who is not actively trying to hide anything, it's another story when it comes to deception.

An even bigger problem is that liars have access to all the same information as would-be lie detectors. If someone knows that touching their face often will be perceived with suspicion, they can simply take care not to do it. In fact, if you are dealing with a person who is very accustomed to lying, or in some way almost believes the story they're telling you, they may show no signs at all.

So, why bother learning to detect lies if it's something that's so difficult to get right? Because there are certain conditions under which lie-detection accuracy *can* improve. If we can understand these conditions and have realistic expectations of our accuracy, we actually become better readers of character and more likely to avoid being deceived.

Lie detecting is generally most accurate when:

- You have a solid baseline of behavior against which to compare current behavior
- The person doing the lying is spontaneous, i.e., they haven't had any

179

time to rehearse their lie or prepare themselves
- The lie comes with real consequences for getting caught—this may up the stakes and make liars more nervous

Unfortunately, there is no single cue or sign that is a reliable indicator of someone's dishonesty. One person may suddenly get more talkative, another may have a little tic they never do otherwise, another may get very serious and distracted. Besides, even if you could reliably spot nervousness, you cannot definitively link it to a lie—the person may just be nervous because they know you distrust them!

We could turn things around and look at it from the other angle—instead of asking how we can become better at spotting deception, can we understand why we get deceived in the first place? From this point of view, nothing much can be done about the existence of liars, but we can certainly look to *ourselves* and ask what aspects of our own personalities, beliefs or behaviors are allowing detection to go unnoticed.

For most people, lying is understood as an absolute moral wrong. We don't like to lie, but we also hate to think that we've been fooled by a liar. If we have an unconscious belief that nobody would really lie to us, or that we could detect it if they did, we are preserving our ego somewhat, and assuring ourselves that the world is largely a just place.

Most people are good and honest, and they simply don't like sitting in judgment of another, preferring the comfort of extending trust—how many of us falsely believe that others will behave with all the same moral scruples as we would?

If we can own our own bias, our expectations and our own unconscious beliefs about what others tell us, we have a better chance at detecting deception. It's nice to imagine that you've got a good radar for liars, and are a gifted "human polygraph machine," but nothing can get in the way of proper observation and analysis as much as the comforting belief that you've done it already. The methods we used in earlier chapters to discover a person's values and personality will need an upgrade if we hope to use them to spot a lie.

It's All About the Conversation

Ask the man in the street how to spot a liar and he may tell you things like, "his eyes go shifty" or "he looks up and to the right" or, "he stutters." Even properly trained professionals may trust some of these techniques as foolproof ways to spot lying. But sadly, if it was this easy, lying would be much less commonplace and nobody would ever be deceived. The truth is, good lie detection goes a lot further than spotting isolated behaviors.

Of course body language matters. But in a way, a lie is a verbal construction—it's a narrative that's presented dynamically, in real time, and always in the context of another person listening in active conversation. Spotting lies is more than just watching like a hawk for a facial twitch here or a sweaty palm there. It's about working with the entire conversation.

In conversation, you are participating, too. You can ask questions, steer the discussion, and subtly put pressure on the person so that *they offer you information*, rather than you having to seek it out. Let's reframe lie-detection as a conversational skill rather than a set of single, static observations.

Your spouse is acting suspicious and you're asking them about where they've been for the last five hours. Your child is telling you a story about how they got their black eye. Or a colleague at work is explaining to you at length why they've decided to drop your project. All of these are living, dynamic conversations, and not simply one-sided performances given on a witness stand.

Your ability to detect a lie will come down to *the way you engage* with the person telling the lie. Your interaction needs to be strategic and proactive. The first thing to keep in mind is to use open ended questions to start off with. Let the other person speak first, and often, to give them time to lay out any possibly conflicting facts or threads you can unravel later to prove a lie.

The appropriately named Dr. Ray Bull of the university of Derby is a criminal investigation professor who has been studying the art and science of this conversational technique for years, publishing papers in multiple psychology, behavior and law journals. His main finding is that it's the *relationship* between the interviewer and interviewee, and the *process* of lie detection, that matters more than anything.

You want to keep your input to a minimum, at least at first. If you have any evidence or information of your own, keep quiet about it for as long as possible. Remember, the liar is in a difficult position. They have to convince you of a story yet they don't usually know what you know. Withholding this information is often enough to get someone to accidentally blurt out something that resolves the issue for you completely.

For a simple example, if your spouse is telling you some long-winded story about how they spent the evening with a friend, ask them a few questions about what they did together, what they ate, what the weather was like at the friend's place, and so on. Watch what they say. At the end of the conversation, you might reveal that you happen to know that that friend is on vacation at the moment, but by not revealing you know this, you give the liar the chance to recite their planned story, and reveal the flaw in their own story.

Watch for how the information is presented in general. Liars will usually offer a complete and highly detailed account all at once, but have little to offer beyond that when questioned. After all, they've rehearsed it all in their heads already, but haven't rehearsed answers to questions they haven't thought of. People telling the truth, however, tend not to come out with everything all at once, but will easily answer when questioned further.

You could try this out directly—suddenly ask a random and unrelated question that the person will definitely not have thought about beforehand. Then notice whether they are floundering to make up something on the spot. Liars also generally take longer to respond to questions and pause more often while narrating their response. Truth-tellers may struggle to remember a detail, but they'll be far more comfortable saying "I don't know" whereas a liar can often be seen to be rushing to make up some detailed nonsense to fill their perceived gap in knowledge.

If you do notice a discrepancy or even a flat out lie, don't let on that you do. Wait a little and watch. You may get to see the liar actively spinning a tale before your eyes. When you eventually do confront such a person with evidence of deceit, continue to watch their response. People caught out in lying may get angry or shut down, whereas a person who is telling the truth may merely act a little confused, and will simply keep repeating the same story.

Dr. James Drikell is the head of the Florida Maxima Corporation, which researches behavioral science issues like deception detection. He has some extra clues on how to analyze the stories of multiple people who may or may not be collaborating on a deception. He claims that when two people are in on a lie together, they don't consult with one another in telling their story, and don't elaborate on the other's telling, whereas truth tellers do. If you suspect two people of lying, watch how they interact with one another—honest people will be far more comfortable and proactive about sharing the story telling.

Use the Element of Surprise

Put yourself in a liar's shoes (or remember the last time you told a whopper!). You have a lot of little details to keep track of, and have to appear calm and confident while doing so. You can imagine that's it's far easier to get your story straight if you've had time to run through everything in detail first. In other words, the more time you have to prepare, the more you can calm your nerves and rehearse your response.

Spontaneous liars are worse liars. If you can arrange it so that you question/talk to the other person on the spur of the moment, you might have a better chance at catching them out in awkward and rushed lying. As with the conversation techniques above, you are not really trying to guess whether the story you are presented with is true or false based solely on body language etc. Rather, you are trying to get the other person to reveal themselves, and to trip up in their own web of deceit.

We've already seen that surprise questions can catch a person off guard, since they take a liar away from their rehearsed script. Watch for any sudden changes in confidence, speed of speech, or eye contact. A classic giveaway is if a person responds to a direct and simple yes/no question with an evasive answer.

This may signal them trying to buy time to think of a convincing lie. A truth teller would have no trouble responding immediately and directly. Repeating the question or offering a long-winded, overly-detailed response is another way to buy time.

For example:

"Hey, someone ate my lunch from the fridge! Mike, did you eat my stuff?"

"Uh, what stuff is that?"

"You know, my lunch. I had it right here. I even had a Post-It note on it . . ."

"Yeah, well, people in this office can be sneaky . . ."

"You ate it, didn't you?"

"Your lunch? Are you calling me a liar?"

"Well, did you?"

"Man, this is rich. I can't *believe* you'd actually suggest . . ."

And so on!

Again, it's all in the *way* the story is presented. When you catch someone off guard, they will be a little flustered all of a sudden, or may even respond with anger. Watch for a sudden shift in mood or speech. Someone might hide their panic by appearing to get angry ("why ask me such a stupid question?" or "What? You don't know?").

If you suspect someone of lying and want to get to the bottom of it, be casual and offhanded, and ask them questions quickly and before they've had time to spin a tale. If you can do this, a lot of behavioral or body language observations might suddenly be more useful—watch for nervousness, or attempts to hide, both physically and verbally.

Some people may suddenly act a little offended, or incur God's protection ("I swear to God!") instead of answering the question directly and plainly. What you want to do is catch a person in a moment of unguardedness and watch their reaction to questions. Very occasionally, a person may be so flustered and embarrassed they immediately confess in a panic.

How to Increase Cognitive Load

Telling the truth is pretty easy—all you have to do is remember what you can and say it out loud. Telling a lie is far harder, cognitively speaking at least. You're not remembering anything, you're actively fabricating a new story—one that has to have sufficient credibility. A great way to get liars to give themselves up is to tax their already overloaded brains until they make a mistake and tell you more obviously what you want to know.

The best approach is not to behave as if you're in a formal interrogation situation, with you playing the role of no-nonsense detective. Rather, be casual but keep the person talking. Listen closely and apply gentle pressure to parts of the story that seem a little thin. In time, the story could unravel or you could find a glaring inconsistency. If you push on this inconsistency, you may be rewarded with even more lies or irreconcilable differences.

A very interesting technique is to begin your conversation by talking directly about how honest the other person feels they are. This cues people to be more honest later on, or at the very least you will uncover a tension between the wish to appear truthful and the act of lying. This tension could push a person to confess on their own or at least fumble their lie.

Canadian researcher Jay Olson has written extensively about the power of persuasion, and it turns out persuasive techniques can be used to great effect when trying to unmask deceptions. It makes sense—you could try and passively detect a lie in another person, or you could actively *massage* the truth out of them using intelligent and targeted questions, tact and persuasion techniques.

When you increase cognitive load, you are essentially giving the other person too much to think about, so their lie falls apart. A useful technique is to actually state something untrue yourself, and watch their response. Not only will this tell you what their baseline behavior is to non-truths, but the extra piece of information will be one more straw on the camel's back. Do this a few times, switching between true and false, and you are asking the liar to juggle a lot on the spot, mentally speaking.

You could also ask them to relay a story you already know to be true, so you can surreptitiously compare their presentation to the possible lie. This is helpful if you don't know the person well but want to get a baseline on their normal behavior.

Ask unexpected questions that will have them temporarily abandoning the rehearsed story. When they come back to it, they may have forgotten the details themselves. Take an inconsequential part of the story and repeat it back to them with an extra piece you added, or a small detail incorrect. See what they do. If they genuinely think you'd just made a mistake, they may go along with the claim for ease.

You've been having normal, natural conversations your whole life—try to see if you can detect any stiffness, awkwardness or unnaturalness in the story presented. If you're far along in the conversation and the cracks are beginning to show, you might even start to directly allude to the consequences of being found lying. This can confuse and stress a person, sapping their cognitive resources and making it more and more likely they'll make a mistake or say something truly damning.

Finally, watch how emotion is expressed during a conversation. Joe Navarro, ex-FBI agent and expert in interrogation, reinforces the importance of clusters of behavior, rather than individual observations. Behind the cognitive fact of the lie, is an *emotion*: guilt, nervousness, fear, or even a secret thrill at getting away with things (called "duper's delight" by those in the know).

Lies can often be presented with a kind of cool, calm detachment. You may see the person carefully add a bit of faked emotion here and there for effect, but if you know them well, these expressions may seem a little off somehow—either the emotion seems delayed, timed strangely, last too long or are of an inappropriate intensity.

This is because the cognitive load that comes with telling a big fib can interfere with genuine expression of emotion. A person struggling to keep up with their own lie will display many of the signs and clues Navarro talks about: pursed lips, angling the body away, touching the neck or face, or ventilating—i.e., doing things to cool off, such as opening the top button of a shirt or brushing hair off the neck and face.

As you increase cognitive load by asking complex and confusing questions, you can expect to see more emotion surfacing. Keep drilling down for specifics. A great way to observe the interplay between emotion and the cognitive load of recounting a fictional narrative, is to ask directly about emotions. Many people rehearse details but don't plan ahead with how they're going to respond emotional (i.e., pretend!).

For example, the FBI agent might ask how someone felt to "discover" a dead body. This might take the person a while to answer (because they didn't build this piece of info into their lie) or they may reply with no emotion or else a very unconvincing display. The truth teller will be able to almost instantly answer in a genuine way, often displaying the same emotion there and then.

Besides asking questions, cognitive overload can be utilized in another way to reveal lying. Because of how much cognitive effort goes into fabricating a narrative and keeping it up, our brain pays less attention to other facets of relaying details. For instance, if a spouse is trying to lie about where they've been the entire day, they will likely narrate their explanation in a way that is devoid of emotion. Details about spending time with friends which would normally be told in a cheerful and happy tone or manner will, when lying, turn into a series of objective statements from which the speaker is detached. This happens because the liar cannot simultaneously be objective in their lie yet emotional when it comes to the details of the lie. As such, try to notice the emotions that a person conveys along with their narrative and analyze whether it really matches what they're saying. Does the narrative seem rehearsed? Would you have been more expressive than them while recounting the same details? Questions like these can help you analyze lying better.

The flip side of this vocal detachment to their narrative is that the emotional cues are then expressed more noticeably in their body language. It is extraordinarily difficult for anyone, even trained liars, to mask certain non-verbal cues when they're lying, and these are the ones you need to detect in clusters to definitively conclude that someone is lying. Some, like facial cues, are more easily hidden. However, studies show that lying produces arousal due to the anxiety and guilt that liars ordinarily experience (unless they're psychopaths). This makes people more susceptible to displaying non-verbal behavioral cues than they normally would be. For instance, people blink more often when they lie because of arousal. Speech disturbances, slips of tongue, pupil dilation, are more signs of lying. Moreover, the frequency of these signs is also directly correlated with the complexity of the lie. So, if a person is blinking a lot more than the average person does, the scale of their lie is probably big too.

Thus, there are two ways you can use cognitive overload to detect lying. You can patiently poke holes into their story by strategically asking the right questions, or you can try to observe specific behavioral cues that accompany lying and cognitive overload. Better yet, use them together to arrive at more accurate conclusions.

General Tips for Better-than-Average Lie-Detecting

- Sit back and let the other person volunteer information, rather than pulling it out of them. Don't let on what you know too early—or at all.
- Stay relaxed and causal. What you are observing is not the person themselves, but the person as they are in a quasi-interrogational situation with *you*. So don't make it seem like an inquisition, otherwise you may simply be watching them feel distressed about the situation itself.
- Don't worry about individual signs and clues like touching the nose, looking up to the right or stuttering. Rather, look at how the person responds in general to *shifts* in the conversation, especially at junctures where you believe they may be having to concoct a story on the fly.
- Listen for stories that seem unusually long or detailed—liars use more words, and they may even talk more quickly.
- Take your time. It may be a while before you uncover a deception. But the longer the other person talks, the more chance they have of slipping up or getting their story tangled.

- Watch primarily for inconsistencies—details of the story that don't add up, emotional expressions that don't fit the story, or abrupt shifts in the way the story is told. Being chatty and then all of a sudden getting quiet and serious when you ask a particular question is certainly telling.
- Always interpret your conversation in light of what you already know, the context, and other details you've observed in your interactions with this person. It's all about looking at patterns, and then trying to determine if any disruptions in that pattern point to something interesting.
- Don't be afraid to trust your gut instinct! Your unconscious mind may have picked up some data your conscious mind hasn't become aware of. Don't make decisions on intuition alone, but don't dismiss it too quickly, either.

Takeaways

- Casual observation of body language, voice and verbal cues can help with understanding honest people, but we need more sophisticated techniques to help us detect liars.

- Most people are not as good at spotting deception as they think they are. Bias, expectation and the belief that we can't or shouldn't be lied to can get in the way of realizing we're being deceived.

- Good lie detection is a dynamic process that focuses on the conversation. Use open ended questions to get people to surrender information voluntarily, and observe. Look out for overly wordy stories that are presented all at once, inconsistencies in the story or emotional affect, delays or avoidance in answering questions, or inability to answer unexpected questions.

- Liars are easier to spot when lying is spontaneous—try not to allow the liar any time to prepare or rehearse a script, or else ask unexpected questions or plant a lie yourself to watch their response and gain a baseline against which to compare the possible lie.

- Increasing cognitive load can cause a liar to fumble their story or lose track of details, revealing themselves in a lie. Keep drilling for detail and be suspicious if details don't add up, if emotion doesn't match content, or if the person is deliberately stalling for time.

- Look out for specific signs that a person is cognitively overloaded. One example is that the liar will display less emotions while speaking than they or an average person normally would in their situation. These emotions will instead leak through in their body language. Most commonly, this manifests in more frequent blinking, pupil dilation, speech disturbances, and slips of tongue.

- Spotting liars is notoriously difficult, but we improve our chances when we focus on strategic and targeted conversations designed to make the liar trip up on his own story, rather than trying to guess hidden intentions from body language alone.

Chapter 5. Using the Power of Observation

In this chapter, we're going to be drawing on much of what we've already covered, but with an extra element: time. With enough time, it's possible to really get to know someone well, whether you're a good reader of people or not. But the truth is we sometimes don't have a lot of time. Sometimes, we need to make quick assessments of people's characters, within a matter of minutes or even seconds.

Here we'll be looking at ways that we can assess people, observe their behavior, hear them speak and, effectively, "cold read" them from scratch, with very few context clues. Everyone has seen the so-called psychics and mediums communicating with the dead. The medium throws out a vague and open-ended cue into the wider audience and sees who picks it up. They then zoom in a little more . . . if the person is on the older side, they make a vague allusion to a child or a spouse, knowing that the majority of people this age will have spouses or children. Depending on their subtle reaction to this tidbit, they narrow in closer still . . .

The spirit of this process is what we're attempting to fine-tune, rather than the outcome (i.e., to deceive people into thinking you're communicating with deceased relatives!). There are in fact some scientifically supported methods for making pretty accurate snap judgments about people—if we know how to use them.

How to Use "Thin Slicing"

In psychology, thin slicing is the ability to find patterns using only very small amounts of data, i.e., "thin slices" of the phenomenon you're trying to observe—in our case, a person and their behavior. A 1992 paper in the *Psychological Bulletin* by psychologists Nalini Ambady and Robert Rosenthal first coined the term, but it's a philosophical and psychological concept that's been around for a while. The idea is to use very few clues to arrive at accurate predictions of future behavior.

Certain psychological studies have shown that the accuracy of people's assessment of others doesn't improve beyond the initial appraisal they make within the first five minutes. This could mean either that first impressions never change, or that people really can gather everything they need to know within just a few moments.

Research by Albrechtsen, Meissner and Susa in 2019 showed that "intuition" (i.e., snap judgments) were in many cases better than chance at identifying bias or deception in others. Interestingly, they also performed better than people who appraised the situation more deliberately and consciously.

Can you draw on this same ability to make better assessments of people around you?

A key aspect of snap judgments is that they're largely unconscious—it's one of the reasons why they can be so quick. Malcolm Gladwell wrote the famous book on thin slicing, *Blink: The Power of Thinking without Thinking*, where he explored these unconscious tendencies. For example, some art experts were able to immediately detect that a new sculpture wasn't quite right somehow, even though they couldn't say why. Later, the sculpture was determined to be a fake.

A famous example is that of John Gottman, who claims to be able to tell with ninety-five percent accuracy whether a couple would still be together in fifteen years, just by looking at them. Curiously, his accuracy actually *dropped* to ninety percent if he spent more time observing the couple—suggesting that the most accurate assessments are made early on.

How can we use thin slicing in our own attempts to better read and understand those around us? Could it really be that intuition and gut instinct outperform our more rational, deliberate and conscious efforts to reason through a decision or judgment?

Yes and no. Nalini Ambady also found that our emotional state could impact the accuracy of these snap judgments: being sad, for example, was shown to lower people's accuracy when assessing others, perhaps because it encourages more deliberate information processing.

Earlier in the book we took pains to examine bias and prejudice, and how these knee-jerk reactions could actually interfere with our ability to read people properly. So, how does the above research feature? Good people-readers typically use *both* processes, and are aware of the fact, using each to offset the potential limitations of the other.

For example, you may interview at a new company and immediately, within the first minute or so, get a "bad feeling" about the person doing the interview and the place in general. You can't say why, but something feels off. You get offered a second interview. You go, and commit to keeping an open mind and gathering as much data as possible, but you hold back on coming to any conclusions just yet. Since you respect your initial gut feeling, you subtly enquire about the role you'll be filling. You are met with evasive body language, some signs of deception and lying, and a story that doesn't quite hold together.

Because of this, you do a little digging and finally a friend in your network tells you that the person just fired from the role you're interviewing for was dismissed for reporting sexual harassment—at the hands of someone who still works there and would eventually be your direct manager. Here, you can see gut instinct and careful, deliberate thinking used together to arrive at a good decision, each informing the other.

Judges use it (often called "court sense"), military and police officers use it, firefighters and first responders use it, and people have used it to find romantic partners, whether they're speed dating or not. Intuition is powerful and often accurate, but if we want to make sure we're not just giving in to unconscious confirmation bias (i.e., looking for "evidence" to prove the snap judgment we've already made and dismissing everything else) then we need to use conscious decision making, too.

When you're dealing with someone new, don't try to think too hard about it right off the bat. Just notice what your knee-jerk reaction is, and allow that to then guide you gently to a deeper and more conscious analysis. Give yourself room to challenge any first impressions, but don't brush off your instinctive response, even if you can't quite explain it!

Making Smart Observations

As you can imagine, the quality of the assessments you make from your thin slice depends a lot on what's in that slice. If someone encountered you one day while you were deep in thought on an intense jog one day, it wouldn't be fair for them to make an entire assessment based on what little data they were met with in those few seconds.

But then, what data *should* you use?

The first few moments you meet someone, allow your brain to do what it does naturally—make snap judgments that fall below the threshold of your conscious awareness. But as you continue, you can draw on more deliberate observational methods. You can slow down your processing and focus deliberately on the things they say, the words they use, the images they share. In the remainder of this chapter, we'll look at whether things like e-mails and social media can really tell us anything about a person, and how to decode not just the way people are speaking, but their actual word choice.

Look at the Words People Use

You're probably already doing this without always being aware of it. Has the way someone has written a text message ever left you thinking less of them? Have you ever been persuaded by someone's particular word choice or guessed someone's mood, education level, gender, or personality just from their e-mail signatures?

A 2006 study published in *Social Influence* found that obscenity and swearing had the effect of making people think the speaker was more intense and persuasive—but interestingly it didn't affect their perceived credibility. A related study in the *Journal of Research in Personality* has found that text message language can tell you a lot about a person, for example more personal pronouns (I, me, mine) correlate with extroversion, neuroticism correlates with negative emotion words and agreeableness with more positive emotion words.

People's word choice can also give you some insight into their mental or physical health. People who tend to be more neurotic use much more evocative phraseology when saying something negative. So for example, if they're annoyed by something, they won't simply state that they dislike the thing that annoyed them. Instead, they'll use harsher language, like saying that they're "sick of" or "hate" that thing. Conversely, more positive people tend to temper their descriptions of things and only seldom use words like hate, disgusting, etc. If you notice that someone is constantly reacting to seemingly minor things with words that indicate acute distress, there's a deeper issue involved.

As we saw in the previous chapter on detecting lies, people who are lying tend not only to show it in their body language, but in the actual spoken words they use, too. Liars tend to speak more (the old "protesting too much") and use more sense words (i.e., to do with seeing, touching etc.) and fewer personal pronouns (perhaps unconsciously distancing themselves or subtly blaming others).

On the ground, this may look like the person who is going to suspicious lengths to tell a convoluted story—a clear sign that the story might be made up. Essentially, the person telling the lie is going to default to stories that are easier to keep track of and relay. They may avoid the use of causal terms (for example, "X did so-and-so because of Y, and that caused Z to happen . . .") since these are slightly more complex to hold in the brain than simply relating a string of events.

Any politician, motivational speaker or marketing expert will tell you that the words you use make a massive difference. But what they do consciously and with intention is something many of us do unconsciously. Our word choice simply emerges from our deeper values, our personalities, our biases, expectations, beliefs, and attitudes.

One thing to watch out for is whether a person uses complex terminology when it isn't explicitly needed. Studies show that people who use atypical words in their everyday conversations without overdoing it tend to be more popular and well-liked because they come across as intelligent. However, if you notice that someone is unnecessarily speaking in jargon when they don't need to, this reflects desperation to be perceived as someone who is smart and knowledgeable. This is useful to know when you're analyzing someone who is in a position of authority, such as a politician, a financial adviser, a boss, etc. If they overuse jargon, you'll know not to trust them, or if they're your boss, to use it to your advantage.

You may also notice a person uses almost exclusively military or hunting terminology when talking about dating—an unconscious admission of how they really view the opposite sex. Someone who is constantly using "we" when they have just met you is trying to tell you something—that they see you as on their side, or at least they want you to be.

On the other hand a person who speaks almost exclusively in "I" statements is showing where their focus really lies. Look at the way that people string together events, or the way they assign cause and effect. For example, someone might say "he got his feelings hurt" instead of saying "I hurt his feelings," telling you how this person sees their own culpability in the situation. Someone who casually tells you that his "old ball and chain is knocked up" is no doubt communicating a very different message than someone who tells you that "we" are expecting.

As you can imagine, this is murky territory, and learning to decode people's word choice is more art than science. You'll need to plug this data into the larger constellation you're trying to build, and take into account local linguistic conventions, age, class, speech impediments, the formality of the context, education levels, or just plain old eccentricity.

But there are guidelines to follow, and avenues to explore. Consider the following questions during your next conversation:

- Does the person use a lot of pronouns or mostly talk about others? Financial analyst Laura Rittenhouse believes that the more times the word "I" occurs in annual shareholder letters, the worse a company's performance overall.
- Are the words very emotional and dramatic or plain, neutral and fact-based only?
- Is there a lot of jargon or technical language? What's its function?
- Does the person use a lot of "$10 words" when simpler terminology would work? Why?

- Does the person swear a lot? What does this tell you about the other data you've gathered?
- What does their vocabulary tell you about the particular model or frame of reference they're using? For example, do they call a disagreement an "attack" or call employees "colleagues"?
- Is the person using words they know you don't understand—or words that only you and they share? Why? Are they creating solidarity and familiarity or trying to exclude you in a power play?
- Are pronouns like you, your, yourself being used to blame, direct attention to someone else, or manipulate?
- Is the person mimicking your language—are they repeating little phrases or words you use? This could be a sign they're seeking agreement and harmony.

Read People like Sherlock Holmes Reads a Crime Scene

We've already seen that we can read a person even when we have access to only small bits of information, such as their voice. In the same way, reading people is something you can do by simply looking at what's right in front of you. Can you join all the dots and *really see* the person behind all these little clues, suggestions, signs?

What better "thin slice" is there than a photograph, a literal snapshot of just one split second in a bigger, fuller life? You can tell enormous amounts about a person by reading their photographs. University of California at Berkley's Dacher Keltner and LeeAnne Harker studied college yearbook photographs of dozens of women, who were all, as you can imagine, smiling.

But there were two different kinds of smiles—a "Duchenne" or genuine smile and a so-called "Pan Am" smile. The genuine smile involved the whole face rising up, with the eyes crinkling closed and lines appearing around the mouth and nose. The posed or forced smile appeared in the mouth alone, and didn't reach up to the eyes or affect the muscles in the rest of the face.

Most interestingly, the researchers caught up with the women in the photographs many years later and found out that those with genuine smiles in their pictures were more likely to be married, to be generally happier, and to enjoy better health than those who had the forced smiles. If *every* picture you see of someone shows them forcing a smile rather than them being genuinely happy, you can obviously conclude that the person is not all that happy (or they're a model, or they hate getting their picture taken—context matters!).

When a psychologist or psychiatrist does an initial interview with a new client, part of their assessment includes physical appearance. It might not seem altogether fair to judge people on their looks in this way, but psychologists are actually looking for very specific things in their observations—is the person unkempt and poorly groomed? Dressed eccentrically or with little regard for the weather or the occasion?

Whether we like it or not, clothing tells us a lot about a person, since none of us dresses neutrally. Our clothing is a way to make an identity claim about who we are and how we want others to see us. It's a powerful way to communicate our sexual and gender identity, our culture, our age, our socio-economic status, our occupations, our unique personalities, and even something like our religious affiliation.

You're probably already doing a lot of appearance-reading already, but try to be a bit more deliberate the next time you meet someone new you'd like to know more about. Psychologist Dr. Jennifer Baumgartner believes there should even be a "psychology of clothing"—how people shop and the clothing they wear tells you a lot about their motivations, values and self-perception. They tell us where we fit in in the world, our status, and the system of meaning we attach to how we look:

- Firstly, forget about any "rules" about what are good clothes, sexy clothes, professional clothes and so on. It's all relative. Instead, look at the person's attire and how it fits with the surrounding environment. A person who insists on wearing fine jewelry and white shoes to a construction site, for example, is sending a clear message about their priorities and values.

- Look at the general level of effort and care. Someone's style may not be to your taste, but notice if they've made an effort or not. Lack of care and attention can signal low self-esteem or depression.

- Look for deliberately chosen markers of status or prestige—is the person making an effort to don a white coat, a uniform, a badge of honor of some kind? What about indicators of wealth or power? This tells you about a person's self-concept and their values.

- Though cultural factors need to be considered, a person who uses clothing to draw attention to their sexuality (especially in inappropriate contexts) is showing you that their sex appeal is a big part of their identity.

- Someone who wears predominantly work clothing, even outside work hours, is communicating that their identity is bound up with what they do for a living. This could apply to stay at home parents, too—a mother who wears sturdy shoes, old tights and a stained hoodie might be not-so-subtly telling you that the needs of her family rank higher than her need to express her individuality!

- More formal dress typically accompanies greater conscientiousness, while wearing darker colors can be an indicator of neuroticism. Plenty of accessories can indicate extroversion (remember the Christmas decorations?).

Home and Possessions—Extensions of the Personality

In rural Provence, France, there is an old tradition of planting either one, two or three cypress trees at the entrance of a home, to signal how willing the occupants are to receive guests. Three trees meant a weary traveler could stop in for some charity and a warm bed, two meant the residents would happily feed and water you, but just one meant to keep your distance.

Communicating to others in this way is not just a French thing, obviously. Some research done in 1989 in the *Journal of Environmental Psychology* suggested that Americans who use exterior Christmas decorations want to convey friendliness and a sense of group cohesion to their neighbors, and tend to be more sociable. If you're visiting someone's home, observe the place as you would observe the manner in which they dressed, their body language, or their word choice—after all, a home is very much an extension of us as people.

Is the house "open" and welcoming? Neatly kept or a little neglected? Look for signs of sociability—guest areas, considerations made for visitors. A person with a bare and overly-clean house may be telling you something about their neuroticism. Someone displaying plenty of expensive décor and gilt framed photographs of themselves with celebrities is telling you what they value—prestige and wealth.

Think of a home as the one place in the world that people feel most comfortable, safe, and themselves. A home—especially more intimate and personal rooms like the bathroom or bedroom—is a space we make our own, in accordance with our needs and values.

Ask yourself, what is there a excessive amount of in a particular space? If a person hangs up a lot of pictures with their family, or has a pile of books in their room, you can easily tell that these are things that matter to them. Alternatively, the absence of things in a house is also a big indicator of someone's personality. Is the furniture too bare bones? Are there very few personal possessions on display? Is there too much empty space in the house? It's possible that the person you're analyzing is simply a minimalist, but these can also be problematic cues that indicate either bad mental health, the lack of social attachments, or generally low self-esteem.

Home is also where we display our aspirations—take note of how people decorate, what they spend money on and what they ignore, and where their inspiration has come from. What do their choices tell you about how they see themselves, or how they might want to be seen by others? Obviously, a person who's only renting for a year may have fewer clues, and a family home may show you the overall family culture more than the individual personalities that make it up, but it's all data!

In Sam Gosling's book *Snoop: What your stuff says about you*, he explains that you can even guess someone's political inclinations from their bedroom décor. He found that American conservatives tended to have more organizational items and conventional décor like flags and sports paraphernalia. Their rooms were better lit and neater than those leaning more liberal, whose bedrooms contained more books and CDs, art supplies, stationary, and cultural memorabilia. Spaces occupied by liberals also tend to be more colorful. Generally, if a space is neat and overly orderly, the occupant is likely to be conservative because they are naturally inclined towards conscientiousness. On the other hand, liberal spaces scream openness and creativity because their occupants do not like being boxed into routine and order.

Naturally, there are pronounced regional differences, and what is seen as tidy or well decorated or modern in one part of the world may be perceived completely differently somewhere else, so it's worth taking this into account. On the other hand, seeing any discrepancies between a home and the local surroundings is a source of information itself—what does it imply when a family wants to build a home that looks nothing like their neighbor's, or adopts customs from a completely foreign country?

According to Gosling, possessions and artifacts can be broken down into roughly three categories:

- Those objects that make **identity claims**—items that show our personality, value or sense of identity directly. Ornaments, posters, awards, photos, jewelry and adornment (think a gold cross around the neck or a Celtic knot tattoo). Look at the space and ask, who lives here? What kind of person owns this item?

- Objects that act as **feeling regulators**—the things that help people manage their own emotional state. An inspirational quote, a picture of a loved one, sentimental items. These all tell you what the person values and cherishes most.

- Finally, items that are **behavioral residues**—these are the things left behind in the ordinary course of life. These could be things like piles of old Vodka bottles in the corner, an unfinished book net to the sofa, a half-finished craft project on the dining room table. These give you a neat glimpse into people's habits and behaviors.

Reading a person's life the way you read their body language or voice is not difficult—it just takes awareness. Observe everything. What radio channels are they listening to in the car, and what are their bumper stickers? What is their username and their chosen desktop wallpaper? Look at wallets, shoes, photographs, sports gear, pets, food and drink consumed, and reading material. These little things can speak volume . . . if you're listening.

How to Read People's Behavior Online

These days, people know not to believe everything they see online, and that the image someone paints of themselves on social media may have very little to do with what they're really like. But is it still possible to look at someone's social media accounts and online behavior and infer a little about who they really are as people? The answer is yes!

First of all, you don't even need to look at social media to begin to get a picture of someone's personality online—start with their e-mails. Besides their word choice and general language (which we've covered

227

earlier), take a peek at the time stamps on when a person usually e-mails you. One or two super late-night e-mails probably doesn't mean anything, but if you consistently receive e-mails in the small hours, you might guess that you're dealing with a night owl.

So what, right? As it happens, a person's chronotype—or their own unique circadian rhythm patterns—can tell you something about their personality. Research by Michael Breus has suggested that those who are early risers but fade before 10 p.m. are more likely to be extroverted, ambitious and socially oriented. Those who are night owls have been found to have slightly higher rates of what are called the "dark triad" personality traits—narcissism, Machiavellianism and psychopathy.

It doesn't mean that the person who texts you late on a Saturday night is a psychopath—rather, that if you have some evidence of a *pattern* of them being a night-owl, they might be more introverted, anxious, and creative. Those who have sleeping schedules that are all over the place are said to have a different chronotype all together; these light sleepers can get stressed out easily, and tend to be more anxious and conscientious than other types.

But back to social media—with hundreds of millions of people using sites like Facebook and Instagram, it would be a shame to ignore this aspect of human behavior. If you're wondering whether you can trust what a person shares on social media to discern anything genuine about them, then you'll be interested in a 2010 study done by Beck and colleagues on students and their social media behavior.

The researchers gave 236 students a personality test to assess their "Big 5" personality traits, and another test designed to measure what their idealized personality was, i.e., a picture of the kind of person they wished they could be. The final piece of the puzzle was to ask strangers to have a look at the students' social media profiles and make some assessments about their personalities.

The perhaps surprising result was that people were actually more likely to display their real, and not idealized, selves on social media. In other words, people were mostly honest and straightforward about who they were on social media. However, the study's findings need to be interpreted with caution—the assessments people made were only in the broadest strokes. Some personality traits are harder to detect on social media. For example, neuroticism can be difficult to see, but conscientiousness and extroversion are more obvious.

So, can social media tell you about a person? For the most part, yes. As with any other information we might analyze to try to understand people, we need to bear in mind that it's only a sliver of data (a thin slice) and that patterns are more important than isolated events. Words can sometimes easily cloud judgment because they are generally tinged with more positive or negative emotion online. However, the kind of pictures a person posts, especially their profile picture, can help you place them somewhat accurately on the Big 5 scale. Studies shows that a person who is high on openness or neuroticism will usually have pictures that includes only them with a facial expression that is neutral instead of positive. People high on conscientiousness, agreeableness, and extroversion are more likely to have pictures with smiles and positive emotions. The latter two categories also generally have more colorful and emotionally loud photos than the other groups.

It's worth remembering, also, that knowing about a person's *idealized* character does actually tell you a lot about their current character. In the same way as a home filled with travel curios and maps on the walls tells you that the person values being well-traveled, social media filled with travel snaps is just a more deliberate way of communicating to others, "I would like you to see me as well-traveled."

Reading People in the Workplace

It's any interviewee's secret dread—that maybe the success of the interview comes down to those crucial few seconds during the initial greeting and handshake, and nothing more. We've seen that first impressions certainly do feature heavily in our assessments of people, and all the old advice seems to hold true. For example, someone's handshake can tell you a lot about them.

A 2011 paper in the journal *Social influence* tried to figure out whether handshakes could help people better judge others. They asked participants to rate the personality of five people after meeting them, with half of participants doing a handshake and the other half no handshake. As it turns out, the group who shook hands were more accurate at assessing conscientiousness in other people than those who didn't shake hands. All those businesspeople who insist on face-to-face meetings may have been onto something all along!

If you're trying to get a read on someone and get the chance to shake their hand, pay attention to those few vital moments: a limp "dead fish" handshake can mean a few things, such as low self-esteem, disinterest, or noncommitment. Sweaty palms can signify anxiety, although not always—some people may just have naturally sweaty palms, so look for corroborating signs.

Look to see who initiates the shake. Those who lean in close and squeeze too hard are trying to control the situation, perhaps even to dominate the meeting somehow. When a person tries to angle their hand so that their palm is facing more to the ground, they are symbolically trying to "get on top" and command the situation, or to control you.

As with hugging, look to see who breaks first from the shake—pulling back immediately is a sign of reluctance or hesitance, while lingering and shaking up and down longer than is comfortable can signify someone trying to persuade or reassure you. If someone offers you a dainty, limp hand for you to shake, almost like a queen would offer her subject to kiss—well, this speaks for itself!

A two handed handshake (a second hand placed over the handshake) is used to demonstrate sincerity, but is actually more likely to be used by politicians or diplomats *attempting* to look sincere—the effect can actually be a little condescending.

Generally, the more open, warm and comfortable the shake, the more extroverted and agreeable the person. Extroversion is the trait most easily detected by handshakes. Even if someone has a handshake that doesn't feel right, however, look to other situational clues before drawing any conclusions.

Interestingly, if you're trying to assess a colleague or potential hire's personality, the advice is to ignore their resume and look at social media. It may not seem fair that people make snap judgments about others' social media accounts, but there is some evidence to suggest it may actually be an accurate method—not just for assessing personality, but also for seeing how someone might perform on the job.

Researcher Don Kluemper asked people to rate the personalities of strangers' social media accounts. He then examined the social media account holders and their overall work performance, finding that those who were perceived to be more conscientious, agreeable and intellectually curious, actually did better in their jobs. We already saw in a previous study that people's self-portrayal on social media is actually quite honest—what this study tells us is that the traits we communicate to others influences everything, including our career performance.

In case you're wondering whether a super casual party picture of someone at the club counts against them, the general finding is that . . . well, context matters. Profiles were rated favorably when they showed people as having broad interests, travel experience, plenty of friends and interesting hobbies— so a student with a few "party pictures" mixed in with everything else might actually be viewed as a well-rounded, authentic person.

At any rate, these studies tell us something important: that some of the most promising sources of insightful information into the people we work with is not where you'd conventionally expect to find it.

Observation can be Active: How to Use Questions

Famous Greek philosopher Aristotle once stated, "Knowing yourself is the beginning of all wisdom," and founding father of the United States of America Benjamin Franklin seemed to espouse similar thoughts: "There are three things extremely hard: steel, a diamond, and to know one's self." One is saying that self-awareness is the root of wisdom, while the other is saying that self-awareness is a difficult state to achieve.

Of course, this book is not necessarily about self-awareness, but we know that the process of gaining self-awareness is similar to getting to read and analyze people better. It's also just as difficult.

This section focuses on what we can discover about others through directly asking them *indirect* questions. From there, we can learn much about people based on their answers. In many ways, it mirrors what we can understand about ourselves through the same process.

How do people typically gain self-awareness? The focus is geared around people asking themselves simple and direct questions that hopefully hint at realizations just outside our conscious knowledge. Typically, they'll ask themselves questions, again, such as "What makes me happy and fulfilled?" Such direct questions should be considered a mediocre starting point, because these questions force you to ramble and create an answer out of nothing. It often doesn't lead to much insight other than pretty platitudes. You might lie or even interpret the question in unhelpful ways.

Seriously, try to answer that previous question in a way that actually gives you some meaning and direction. What about if you were asked something like, "What parts of your week do you look forward to the most" or "What would you do if you won the lottery and could choose how to spend your time?" or "What is your favorite type of long-term vacation?" These questions elicit concrete answers—specific pieces of you or other people—that you can work with and seek to delve into. Really, we are asking about people's behaviors, which provide the best basis for understanding people. Thoughts and intentions are important, but ultimately, if they are never translated into action, they are useless for our purposes.

And really, this is the introduction to how to analyze pieces of information from people that are ambiguous and not definitive by nature.

Indirect Questions; Direct Information

And so this chapter provides a novel way to analyze people. Through innocent questioning, we can uncover a host of information that represents an entire worldview or set of values. For instance, what if you were to ask someone where they obtained their news and which television channel, which set of publications, which magazines, and which pundits or hosts they preferred? It's a prime illustration of an indirect question that lets you understand quite a bit about how they think. It involves a bit of extrapolation and guesswork, but at least there's a concrete piece of information to go on and many concrete associations with it.

We start this chapter with some of these indirect questions before going even more in-depth by asking people for stories and seeing what we can glean from those. These questions are phrased to challenge and inspire deep thought. They ask people to dive deeper such that we can begin to understand their behavioral and thought patterns.

1. What kind of prize would you work hardest for, and what punishment would you work hardest to avoid?

The answer to this question might help identify the true motive behind an individual's drive. Beyond surface-level things, what is really motivating people? What do they really care about? And what type of pain or pleasure matters to them? On an instinctual level, what really matters the most in both a positive and negative way? In a way, this answer also reflects values.

For example, gamblers all want one prize: the jackpot. They try and try again, whether it be with scratchers or slot machines to try and win the big prize money. Are they motivated by winning back their losses? Is their hope to become richer than they can imagine? Do they actually want it, or are they filling a void and keeping themselves distracted?

Why are they working so hard? You might surmise that their motivation is the thrill and rush of the risk involved. Do they care about making steady pay or finding their purpose? Maybe, and maybe not. When you can dig into what someone wants the most and why, you can often find what is driving them without having to ask it directly. The way people answer this question will clearly tell you their priorities and what they consider pain and pleasure in their lives.

Look for the emotion behind people's answers here, and you can get a pretty good read on their values. A goal of rising to CEO-level doesn't just exist in a vacuum—what are the feelings, emotions, and fulfilled expectations that come from wanting it? Likewise, wanting to avoid being poor speaks to very specific desires for security and safety from danger.

2. Where do you want to spend money, and where do you accept skimping on or skipping altogether?

This answer reveals what matters to someone's life and what they want to experience or avoid. This is not really about the item or items to be purchased; there comes a point where material belongings no longer have a use, and it's about what those items represent and provide. For example, sometimes, spending money on experiences instead of a new purse has the potential to improve someone's overall well-being and outlook on life. Again, look for the underlying emotions and motivations behind the answer.

So what do you have no problem splurging on, and what doesn't matter to you? For instance, when deciding on vacation expenditures, people may opt to splurge on an epic boat excursion and stay in a shabby hotel. This reveals their desire to experience an unforgettable moment rather than staying in a nice hotel with golden toilets, which they view as a waste of money. Others might opt for the opposite and revel in their creature comforts while not seeing much of the scenery. In either case, they've used their money to quite literally identify and spend toward their priorities and values.

Where your money goes is an important part of what makes you happy, so if you can pay attention to where you let it flow and where you cut it off, you'll immediately know what matters to you on a daily basis. Contrast this question to if you were to ask someone, "What do you value in your daily life?" Again, there is a concrete answer here to analyze.

This same principle applies equally to time, money, and effort. Where these things flow, whether consciously or unconsciously, represents the values people possess.

3. What is your most personally significant and meaningful achievement and also your most meaningful disappointment or failure?

It's common that experiences, whether they're good or bad, shape people into who they are. Achievements and failures tie into how someone sees oneself. Significant experiences also tend to create their self-identities—*you are this kind of person because you did this and succeeded or failed*. We can't escape the fact that past occurrences will often influence our current and future actions. They don't have to, but this isn't a book about changing your mindsets. The point is that large events will reverberate throughout our entire lives.

So this question will get a response about how people view themselves, for better or worse. Failure will painfully poke perceived flaws they hate about themselves, while achievements will bring up the strengths they are proud of.

A career woman who has worked her way up the corporate ladder might proudly reflect on her accomplishment. Why does she consider this her greatest achievement? Because she values independence, resilience, and determination, and that's exactly what it takes to get to that career pinnacle. She looks back to the things she did in order to get that corner office, and she feels positively about them.

Thus, the answer about her career accomplishments is actually a story about the positive traits she utilized in reaching that point—her self-identity. You can imagine that the same negative type of self-identity might unfold if the same woman were to talk about her failures and ended up in a job that she despised. Those are the exact things she hates the most.

The way that people answer this question shows who they want to be, and this is reflected in exactly how their expectations have either been fulfilled or not.

4. What is effortless and what is always exhausting?

This is a question that is designed to better understand what people actually enjoy. Something that is effortless isn't always an innate talent, but rather an indication that they enjoy it. On the other hand, something that is always exhausting is not always about people's lack of competency, but rather a distaste for the actual activity. Thus, answers to this question can indicate where people find natural joy and enjoyment, even if they don't realize it themselves.

For instance, as a baker answers this question, she may recognize her rather mediocre capacity for creativity for blending ingredients together to make a dessert. Although she is above average, she is not naturally talented at it, and it has been very difficult for as long as she can remember. She was not innately talented with culinary creativity, and yet she finds joy in it such that she is always driven to it.

It's challenging but effortless in a way that she doesn't grow tired of.

On the other hand, she may have a natural talent in understanding and following traditional recipes—yet it is not something that she values or particularly cares about. If we were to look at only her innate talents, we would conclude that she should stick to only executing the dishes of others. But it's simply not what she values. As mentioned previously, wherever our time, effort, energy, and money goes, such are our values.

5. If you could design a character in a game, what traits would you emphasize and which would you ignore?

This question asks what people see as their ideal self and also what they feel is less important in the world. Imagine that you have a limited number of points to give a person but six traits to spread the points across. Which will you choose to emphasize and bolster, and which will you choose to leave average or even lacking?

Suppose you have the ability to choose between the traits of charisma, academic intelligence, sense of humor, honesty, resilience, and emotional awareness. The traits you'd choose to put the maximum number of points in is how you'd like others to see you. It may represent your current composition of traits, or it might be completely opposite to who you currently are. In either case, it's more than likely that this either represents how you see yourself or how you would like to see yourself. And the other traits? Well, they simply matter less. In turn, they seek out people with those traits they like and are less keen to seek out those with the other traits. There are probably stories behind each of the traits that people might choose as well.

A related question to ask others is, "What traits are common in other people?" This question comes from a 2010 psychological study by Dustin Wood, in which he found that people tended to describe others with similar traits as themselves. Presumably this is because people tend to see their own qualities in others. No one believes that their mental makeup of traits is uncommon, and thus, they believe everyone has a similar perspective and way of thinking as them. Answers to this question are a direct insight into what traits people believe they have, for better or worse. From there, you know what kind of approach they have to the world—kind, generous, distrusting, mischievous, or even ill-spirited.

6. What charity would you donate millions to if you had to?

Answering this question forces one to answer what they care about in the world at large rather than just in their own life.

Will you donate to an animal shelter or a charity for cancer? Perhaps you would sponsor a child from a third-world country? They all say very different things. You might have had a first- or secondhand experience with any of these causes. Whatever the case, it shows what matters when people start to think outside of themselves. You can see a whole sector of the world that they are concerned about, and this allows you to see how they view their place in the world. In other words, whose interests do they tend to prioritize or be motivated by? As always, look to the underlying emotion.

Being able to ask these questions evokes a deeper connection to people's values, ideas, and awareness. The purpose of asking these is to, again, examine behavior. These questions guide a person in thinking about the most relevant aspects of his or her character. They also make people think beyond predictable statements and organically stimulate more meaningful thought. Look beyond the answers and read between the lines. Critical thinking, evaluation, and reflection are the key skills at play here.

Next, we go deeper by asking people for stories that they construct, rather than just a relatively short answer, to see what we can glean from hearing their internal dialogue in full effect.

7. *What animal best describes you?*

The great thing about this question is that it's a very personal inquiry hidden in plain sight. People are far more comfortable talking about certain traits they admire in others than they are about talking directly about themselves. You might also find that asking this question has people feeling very willing to share revealing information that they otherwise might have felt too uncomfortable to reveal.

Something about the distance that's created when talking about an animal can prompt some very forthright and honest answers. People may inadvertently tell you about who they *wish* they were when they tell about their favorite animal. Listen carefully to the person who says they love dogs but dislike cats. Ask them why, and their answer will tell you plainly about the traits they value in others, in themselves, and how they wish to be.

The best way to pose this question is as casually as possible. Don't make it seem like you're grilling for a serious answer— ironically, this attitude will quickly reach past people's defenses and have them blurting out information about themselves that can be incredibly meaningful. What they tell you immediately after is important—whatever is top of their mind is the aspect of themselves they likely see as most important, most relevant or most fixed.

For example, a person immediately tells you they're a bear and needs no further prompting for them to explain to you why: they're fierce, protect their loved ones and shouldn't be messed with. But if they didn't choose a shark, could this mean that they also see themselves as having a bit of "cuddly" side to them, too?

On the surface, such questions can seem innocent and playful, but it's this very simplicity that allows people to respond most honestly—as though to a Rorschach test. Did they choose a carnivore or an herbivore? A mythical animal? A pest? A domesticated animal or a wild, slightly dangerous one? Such a question adds immense depth and color to your understanding of the person—and it does so in their own terms.

8. What's your favorite movie?

This is perhaps as obvious on the surface as the previous one, but many people don't stop to truly think about the huge amounts of information they're being offered when people share things like their favorite films. With this question, people are really sharing with you the narratives and stories they're drawn to, which in turn show you in a deep way what their inner moral universe looks like, how they think of the good and bad guys, or even how they envision their own grand story as it unfolds.

What is it about a particular film that they like? Don't simply assume that they identify with the main character—it may be the director or the genre itself that most powerful speaks to them. And if someone answers, "Well, it's a very obscure independent Polish film released in the early 40s. I don't expect you know anything about it," you can infer a lot even though you've never heard of the film! You can assume that this person values exclusivity and rarity, and likes to style themselves a connoisseur with excellent taste (i.e., what other people would identify as an infuriating hipster!).

Use the answer to this question along with other data you're gathering. What does it mean that the shy, skinny kid in the corner best loves a superhero film? What would a retired Japanese mom see in a serious film about the slave trade in the deep south? The person who tells you their favorite film is a comedy—does it mean anything that the comedy they choose is not a recent one, but one from decades past, that would have been popular when they were just a child?

9. What would you rescue from a fire in your home?

You know the drill. Your entire home is burning and you can only go in to fetch one single treasured item, no more. This is another question that taps deeply into a person's most fundamental values and priorities. Maybe you had a particular person pegged as a pragmatic, almost emotionally-stunted person until they tell you they'd save a single book of poetry.

Crisis and emergency situations have a way of quickly cutting through the clutter of life. People may appear a certain way right up until their backs are against the wall. In the film *Force Majeure*, a family finds themselves facing a terrifying but brief threat—an oncoming avalanche. In the few heated moments, the father fleas the scene, saving himself, while the mother stays with her children. Though the danger passes and everyone is soon safe again, the rest of the movie explores what the father's actions mean—did his knee-jerk response in the moment say something about what he really valued—i.e., himself, and not his family?

Try to understand not just what a person would save, but why. A person who would quickly grab their pet cat before anything else is telling you that they value life more than inanimate possessions. A person who grabs their passport is telling you that they see their freedom to move, their ability to travel, as a very special thing.

Similarly, someone who simply tells you they'd grab their wallet because they had all their money, cards and driver's license in there is also telling you something important—that they are interpreting your question not in terms of values or hypotheticals, but as a literal and practical dilemma to be solved in the most logical way possible. Very different from the person who boldly claims they would save an old photograph of their great-great-grandmother!

10. What scares you most?

Many of the above questions are focused on values, principles, priorities, desires. But of course, you can also learn a lot about a person by what they actively avoid, detest and fear. This tells you not only what they do value, but also how they see themselves. After all, it makes sense that you would fear the thing you most felt unable to protect yourself against, or the thing that you felt was most harmful to you personally. This can yield enormous amounts of insight into how a person sees their own strengths and limitations.

Someone who says "spiders" is going to have a very different psychological makeup than someone who claims, "early onset dementia, where I gradually forget who I am and the faces of everyone I used to love." Fears are often a door to people's most firmly held principles—a person who is extremely morally-inclined and driven by justice and fairness might fear serial-killers, psychopaths or even demonic supernatural entities.

On the other hand, fears can also tell you what that person thinks of their ability to handle adversity or suffering. The person who fears rejection, abandonment and criticism is telling you that in their world, psychological harm is more serious than physical harm. Likewise, what would you infer about someone who unflinchingly tells you, "I'm not scared of anything"?

Takeaways

- There is a wealth of information we can observe and analyze when trying to understand other people, but we usually don't have a lot of time to do it. Using small amounts of data to make accurate assessments is called "thin slicing." Snap decisions based on thin slicing can be surprisingly accurate. A good technique is to trust your initial unconscious reactions (intuition) but supplement this with more deliberate observations after the fact.

- Note the words people use in their texts and e-mails, for example their use of pronouns, active/passive voice, swearing, accent, word choice and so on. Also note how emotionally charged someones words are, and if this amount is appropriate to the context they are used in. For example, using overly negative language in seemingly benign situations can be an indicator of bad mental health or low self-esteem

- Read a person's home and possessions like you would their body language and voice: examine the closedness or openness of a home to determine sociability, for example. Notice both, what there is an excess of and what is conspicuously lacking in the spaces one occupies frequently. Personal possessions can make identity claims, can speak to the way a person regulates their own emotions, or can be evidence of certain past behaviors or habits.

- You can also rely on people's behavior online to discern what kind of person they are, albeit some caution is necessary here. Pay attention to what kind of pictures people post and the emotions they convey, especially whether they are positive, neutral, or negative. People who post positive pictures are more likely to be agreeable, extroverted, or conscientious, whereas people with more neutral photos are generally higher on openness and neuroticism.
- You can use questions to actively elicit very useful information. Hypothetical questions can get around people's defenses and have them honestly revealing insightful information straight away. This helps you get a better handle on their

secret desires, values and self-perception.

Summary Guide

INTRODUCTION

- Most of the communication that
  takes place between people is nonverbal in nature. What people say is
  often a poor indicator of what they
  want to convey, which makes people-
  reading a valuable life skill with
  almost endless benefits. Although
  we're all blessed with different
  aptitudes, it's possible to develop this
  skill in ourselves, as long as we can
  be honest about where we're starting
  from.
- No matter which theory of model we
  use to help us analyze and interpret
  our observations, we need to
  consider context and how it factors
  in. One sign in isolation rarely leads
  to accurate judgments; you need to
  consider them in clusters. The
  culture people come from is another

important factor that helps contextualize your analysis appropriately.

- Behavior is meaningless in a void; we need to establish a baseline so that we know how to interpret what we see. This means that you need to ascertain what someone is normally like to detect deviances from that to draw accurate interpretations of when they're happy, excited, upset, etc.

- Finally, we become great people-readers when we understand ourselves. We need to know what biases, expectations, values, and unconscious drives we bring to the table so we are able to see things as neutrally and objectively as possible. We must refrain from letting pessimism cloud our judgments because its often easier to arrive at the more negative conclusion when an alternate, more positive one is equally likely.

- To gain better insight into the progress you make as you read through this book, you need to know your proficiency at analyzing people as you start out. Simon Baron Cohen has come up with a test available on http://socialintelligence.labinthewild .org/ that'll help you gauge how good you are at reading people's emotions right now. It is also a good way to come to the realization that we are perhaps not as good at reading people as we think we are.

CHAPTER 1. MOTIVATION AS A BEHAVIORAL PREDICTOR

- We've talked about analyzing and predicting behavior based on people's emotions and values, but what about motivation? It turns out there are a few prominent and fairly universal models of motivation that can give you a helpful framework to understand people with. When you can pinpoint what people are motivated by, you can see how everything leads back to it either directly or indirectly.

- Any discussion on motivation must begin with the pleasure principle, which generally states that we move toward pleasure and move away from pain. If you think about it, this is omnipresent in our daily lives in both minuscule and huge ways. As such, this actually makes people more predictable to understand. What is the pleasure people are seeking, and what is the pain they are avoiding? It's always there in some way.
- Next, we move to the pyramid of needs, otherwise known as Abraham Maslow's hierarchy of needs. It states that we are all seeking various types of needs in various points in our lives; when you can observe which level other people are in, you can understand what they are seeking out and motivated by. The levels of the hierarchy are as follows: physiological fulfillment, safety, love and belonging, self-esteem, and self-actualization. Of course, this model, as well as the next one, also functions based on the pleasure principle.
- Finally, we come to defense of the ego. This is one of our most powerful

motivators, but it is mostly unconscious. Simply put, we act to guard our ego from anything that would make us feel psychologically *less*. In doing so, it is so powerful that it allows us to bend reality and lie to ourselves and others—all outside of our conscious awareness. Defense mechanisms are the ways that we avoid responsibility and negative feelings, and they include denial, rationalization, projection, sublimation, regression, displacement, repression, and reaction formation, to name a few. When you know the ego is in play, it often takes front stage over other motivations.

CHAPTER 2. THE BODY, THE FACE, AND CLUSTERS

- Finally, we get right into the thick of it. How can we read and analyze people just through sight and observation? We cover two primary aspects: facial expressions and body language. It's important to note that though many aspects have been scientifically proven (with physiological origins), we can't say that simple observations are foolproof. It can never be definitive because there are too many external factors to take into account. But we can better understand what typical things to look for and what we can glean from them.

- We use two types of facial expressions: micro- and macroexpressions. Macroexpressions are larger, slower, and more obvious. They are also routinely faked and consciously created. Microexpressions are the opposite of all of those things: incredibly quick, almost unperceivable, and unconscious. Psychologist Paul Ekman identified a host of microexpressions for each of the six basic emotions and in particular has also identified microexpressions to indicate nervousness, lying, or deception.
- Body language has a much broader range of possible interpretations. Generally, a relaxed body takes up space, while an anxious body contracts and wants to conceal and comfort itself.

There are too many specifics to list in a bullet point, but just keep in mind that the only true way to analyze body language is to first know exactly what someone is like when they are normal.

- To put everything together, we need to read the body as a whole, and look for general clusters of behavior that work together to communicate a unified message. The voice can be thought of as a part of the body, and read like other body language. Look for signs or cues that are incongruent and don't mesh well with the other cues they're giving, this might reveal that the other person is trying to hide something if you can notice other cues that reaffirm this conclusion. However, as always, the signs you've picked up on could well be meaningless, so make sure you have enough data to support them.

CHAPTER 3. PERSONALITY SCIENCE AND TYPOLOGY

- We start our journey into analyzing people like a psychologist by first taking a look at the various personality tests and seeing what we can glean from them. It turns out, quite a bit, although they can't be said to be definitive measures or categories of people. Mostly, they provide different scales and perspectives through which to view people differently.
- The Big Five personality traits are one of the first attempts to classify people based on specific traits rather than as a whole. You can remember the traits easily with the acronym OCEAN: openness to experience (trying new things), conscientiousness (being cautious and careful), extroversion (drawing energy from others and social situations), agreeableness (warm and sympathetic), and neuroticism (anxious and high-strung).
- Next, the MBTI, though helpful as a guideline, can sometimes suffer from people treating it like a horoscope and reading into their type what they wish to see about themselves. The MBTI

functions on four distinct traits and how much of each trait you are or are not. The traits are generally introverted/extroverted (your general attitude toward others), intuitive/feeling (how you perceive information), thinking/feeling (how you process information), and perceiving/judging (how you implement information). Thus, this creates sixteen distinct personality types.

- The MBTI does suffer from some shortcomings, including the usage of stereotyping to classify people, and the lack of consistency when people score differently depending on their current moods and circumstances.

- The Keirsey temperaments are a way of organizing the same information gleaned from the MBTI. Here, there are four distinct temperaments, each with two types of roles instead of sixteen personality types. The four temperaments are guardian, artisan, idealistic, and rational. Keirsey estimated that up to eighty percent of the population fell into the first two temperaments.

- Finally, the Enneagram is the final personality test we cover in this chapter. It is composed of nine general types of personalities: reformer, helper, achiever, individualist, investigator, loyalist, enthusiast, challenger, and peacemaker. Each type is composed of a specific set of traits, and in this way, it functions more similarly to Keirsey's temperaments.

CHAPTER 4. LIE DETECTION 101 (AND CAVEATS)

- Casual observation of body language, voice and verbal cues can help with understanding honest people, but we need more sophisticated techniques to help us detect liars.
- Most people are not as good at spotting deception as they think they are. Bias, expectation and the belief that we can't or shouldn't be lied to can get in the way of realizing we're being deceived.

- Good lie detection is a dynamic process that focuses on the conversation. Use open ended questions to get people to surrender information voluntarily, and observe. Look out for overly wordy stories that are presented all at once, inconsistencies in the story or emotional affect, delays or avoidance in answering questions, or inability to answer unexpected questions.
- Liars are easier to spot when lying is spontaneous—try not to allow the liar any time to prepare or rehearse a script, or else ask unexpected questions or plant a lie yourself to watch their response and gain a baseline against which to compare the possible lie.
- Increasing cognitive load can cause a liar to fumble their story or lose track of details, revealing themselves in a lie. Keep drilling for detail and be suspicious if details don't add up, if emotion doesn't match content, or if the person is deliberately stalling for time.
- Look out for specific signs that a person is cognitively overloaded. One example is that the liar will display less emotions

while speaking than they or an average person normally would in their situation. These emotions will instead leak through in their body language. Most commonly, this manifests in more frequent blinking, pupil dilation, speech disturbances, and slips of tongue.

- Spotting liars is notoriously difficult, but we improve our chances when we focus on strategic and targeted conversations designed to make the liar trip up on his own story, rather than trying to guess hidden intentions from body language alone.

CHAPTER 5. USING THE POWER OF OBSERVATION

- There is a wealth of information we can observe and analyze when trying to understand other people, but we usually don't have a lot of time to do it. Using small amounts of data to make accurate assessments is called "thin slicing." Snap decisions based on thin slicing can be surprisingly accurate. A good technique is to trust your initial unconscious reactions (intuition) but supplement this with more deliberate observations after the fact.

- Note the words people use in their texts and e-mails, for example their use of pronouns, active/passive voice, swearing, accent, word choice and so on. Also note how emotionally charged someones words are, and if this amount is appropriate to the context they are used in. For example, using overly negative language in seemingly benign situations can be an indicator of bad mental health or low self-esteem

- Read a person's home and possessions like you would their body language and voice: examine the closedness or openness of a home to determine sociability, for example. Notice both, what there is an excess of and what is conspicuously lacking in the spaces one occupies frequently. Personal possessions can make identity claims, can speak to the way a person regulates their own emotions, or can be evidence of certain past behaviors or habits.

- You can also rely on people's behavior online to discern what kind of person they are, albeit some caution is necessary here. Pay attention to what kind of pictures people post and the emotions they convey, especially whether they are positive, neutral, or negative. People who post positive pictures are more likely to be agreeable, extroverted, or conscientious, whereas people with more neutral photos are generally higher on openness and neuroticism.

- You can use questions to actively elicit very useful information. Hypothetical questions can get around people's defenses and have them honestly revealing insightful information straight away. This helps you get a better handle on their secret desires, values and self-perception.

Printed in the USA
CPSIA information can be obtained
at www.ICGtesting.com
LVHW022041031223
765573LV00039B/816